THIS IS NO LONGER THE PROPERTY
OF THE SEATTLE PUBLIC LIBRARY

P9-EDA-775

Everything Is Broken Up
and Dances

ALSO BY EDOARDO NESI

Story of My People
Infinite Summer

EVERYTHING IS BROKEN UP AND DANCES

The Crushing of the Middle Class

GUIDO
MARIA BRERA

EDOARDO
NESI

TRANSLATED FROM THE ITALIAN BY
ANTONY SHUGAAR

OTHER PRESS ⟨⟩ NEW YORK

Copyright © 2017 La nave di Teseo, Milano

Originally published in Italian as *Tutto è in frantumi e danza*
in 2017 by La nave di Teseo, Milan.

English translation copyright © 2017 Antony Shugaar

Epigraph republished with permission of Henry Holt & Company from
The Apocalypse of Our Time by Vasily Rozanov, 1977; permission conveyed
through Copyright Clearance Center, Inc.

Production editor: Yvonne E. Cárdenas
Text designer: Julie Fry
This book was set in Bembo and Bodoni by
Alpha Design & Composition of Pittsfield, NH.

1 3 5 7 9 10 8 6 4 2

All rights reserved. No part of this publication may be reproduced
or transmitted in any form or by any means, electronic or mechanical,
including photocopying, recording, or by any information storage
and retrieval system, without written permission from Other Press LLC,
except in the case of brief quotations in reviews for inclusion in a
magazine, newspaper, or broadcast. Printed in the United States of America
on acid-free paper. For information write to Other Press LLC,
267 Fifth Avenue, 6th Floor, New York, NY 10016. Or visit our Web site:
www.otherpress.com

Library of Congress Cataloging-in-Publication Data
Names: Brera, Guido Maria, author. | Nesi, Edoardo, 1964– author. |
Shugaar, Antony, translator.
Title: Everything is broken up and dances : the crushing of the middle class /
Guido Maria Brera and Edoardo Nesi ; translated by Antony Shugaar.
Other titles: Tutto è in frantumi e danza. English
Description: New York : Other Press, 2018.
Identifiers: LCCN 2017056723 (print) | LCCN 2017042772 (ebook) |
ISBN 9781590519318 (hardback) | ISBN 9781590519325 ()
Subjects: LCSH: Economic development—Italy—History—20th century. |
Liberalism—Italy—History—20th century. | Italy—Economic conditions—
8/20th century. | Italy—Economic conditions—21st century. | Globalization—
Economic aspects—Italy. | Political culture—Italy. | BISAC: BUSINESS &
ECONOMICS / Development / Economic Development. | BIOGRAPHY &
AUTOBIOGRAPHY / Cultural Heritage. | BUSINESS & ECONOMICS /
International / General.
Classification: LCC HC305.B83413 2018 (ebook) | LCC HC305 (print) |
DDC 330.9/051—dc23
LC record available at https://lccn.loc.gov/2017056723

To those who still believe, and those who wish to stay

The show is over.
The audience get up to leave their seats.
Time to collect their coats and go home.
They turn round.
No more coats and no more home.

—Vasily Rozanov

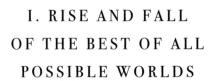

I. RISE AND FALL
OF THE BEST OF ALL
POSSIBLE WORLDS

AMERICA'S MILLENNIUM GALA

ON DECEMBER 31, 1999, Bill and Hillary Clinton held a series of public and private events in Washington under the general heading of "America's Millennium: A Celebration for the Nation," which included, in particular, the presentation of a time capsule, a gala reception at the White House, and a concert at the Lincoln Memorial followed by a fireworks show that Will Smith, emcee for the evening, described in the following words: "A fireworks display like we've never seen…like, *ever* in history!"

The time capsule contained objects and documents that, for whatever reason, were considered especially well suited to speak for the present and the past of the United

States of America: Ray Charles's sunglasses, the Hawaiian state flag, photos of Earth from outer space, a computer chip, a cell phone, Corningware, the Bill of Rights, a helmet from World War II, a video of the moon landing, *The Grapes of Wrath* by Steinbeck, letters from students, a model of the DNA double helix, the eighty-five-letter Cherokee alphabet, a recording of the sound of Louis Armstrong's trumpet, various books by Faulkner, a photograph of Rosa Parks, a model of the Liberty Bell, children's art, broadcasts of the Metropolitan Opera, a section of transoceanic cable, an origami eagle, a piece of the Berlin Wall, and a CD-ROM of the Human Genome Project.

Five hundred people attended the reception at the White House—more guests than had ever attended a White House event, according to newspaper accounts of the time—and packed the rooms and gardens of the presidential residence. Among the guests were Sophia Loren, Jack Nicholson, Muhammad Ali, Slash, Bono, the astronaut John Glenn, Carl Lewis, John McCain, Diane Keaton, Jesse Jackson, Mary Tyler Moore, Robert De Niro, Robert Rauschenberg, Martin Scorsese, Dave Brubeck, Liz Taylor, and many others. The guests were served an array of foods that included Beluga caviar, lobsters, oysters, truffle-marinated rack of lamb, and a chocolate and champagne mousse, all washed down with American wines.

After dinner, the guests at the reception were whisked to the Lincoln Memorial, for the millennium concert—probably the only concert in history where the singers performed in formal attire, because they came directly from the White House. It was a cavalcade of aging superstars — clearly the Clintons' favorites — and a few young superstars singing in the style of the older superstars. Tom Jones performed "It's Not Unusual," Kenny Rogers did "The Gambler," two members of Foreigner sang "I Wanna Know What Love Is," Don McLean sang "American Pie," Celine Dion belted out "My Heart Will Go On," the love theme from *Titanic*, in a live, worldwide broadcast, and so on.

Between the various performances, there were speeches.

Standing behind a lectern, Hillary made a brief and chilly reference to the American Dream, quoting both Martin Luther King Jr. and John F. Kennedy Jr., while John McCain spoke of the contribution to the nation made by the American military, quoting Ronald Reagan.

A celebratory film was shown that had been shot for the occasion by Steven Spielberg, summarizing the saga of American and world cinema. It takes a special effort to forgive the shovelsful of rhetoric beneath which the director buried the magnificent story of a century that's impossible to summarize.

At last came Bill Clinton's moment, following an introduction by Will Smith in a broad-brimmed black hat; Smith couldn't resist the solemnity of the occasion, respectfully emphasizing every syllable of his "Ladies and gentlemen, the President of the United States."

He spoke, *the President of the United States* did, and he seemed strangely unwise as he brought to an end the American century — for that matter, Clinton has never seemed wise—but he certainly did seem sanguine, strong, confident, authoritative, and proud. Satisfied. A perfect portrait of the America of that time. The America that was living through the last few years of the longest period of peace and prosperity in its history. His America.

He said: "We Americans must not fear change. Instead, let us welcome it, embrace it, and create it."

He said that his countrymen would need to learn "to share with our fellow Americans and, increasingly, with our fellow citizens of the world the economic benefits of globalization, the political benefits of democracy and human rights, the educational and health benefits of all things modern, from the Internet to the genetic encyclopedia to the mysteries beyond our solar system." He said: "We may not be able to eliminate all the harsh consequences of globalization, but we can communicate more and travel more and trade more, in a way that lifts the lives of ordinary working families everywhere and the quality of our global environment."

He even counseled the importance of "unlock[ing] secrets from global warming to the black holes in the universe ..." and concluded his five-minute speech in a minor key, graciously, so sure of himself and the righteousness of his time as president that he didn't feel the need to add so much as a crumb of emphasis to the moment: in the new millennium everything would change and new challenges would have to be met, of course, but there could be no doubt that America would be capable of rising to all those occasions.

He even trotted out the none-too-evocative and hardly original imagery of a torch just passed to a new century of young Americans, and had the good taste to fall silent a few seconds before midnight, allowing the audience to focus on the illumination of the great obelisk of the Washington Monument, perfectly timed to coincide with the last few seconds of the millennium, and the fireworks show that followed, a show that, at least to view it now on a computer screen, doesn't look all that wonderful.

From the video clips that can be found online, it's hard to figure out whether Bono sings before or after Clinton's speech, and therefore before or after the beginning of the celebrations proper for the new millennium, but the fact remains that Quincy Jones introduces him to thunderous applause from the tens and tens of thousands of people clustering around the Reflecting Pool—the pool, just to be specific, where Forrest Gump's girlfriend wades and dances—and Bono appears atop the Lincoln Memorial's staircase without his usual swagger, his guitar slung over his shoulders.

There's a brief hug with Quincy Jones, a quick smile toward the orchestra and Daniel Lanois—U2's record producer and an excellent performer, already onstage waiting for Bono, perched on a stool and holding an electric guitar—and as we hear the opening notes of "One," Bono says: "I've come here tonight to pay respect to an administration and a president who has made history over the last year. As an Irishman, we have peace in Ireland.

That is unimaginable without Bill Clinton, Senator George Mitchell, and Sandy Berger, so I pay respect to them...And globally, I pay respect to the American people, Democrats and Republicans who came together this year, to establish a principle...a principle which has forever altered the relationship between the haves and the have-nothings on the planet...I don't know how many of you know that the United States has canceled its debts owed by thirty-six of the poorest countries on earth...It's a big deal, thank you...At a time of your prosperity, I am thankful and I ask you not to forget your roots and your humble origins...The Scriptures call for this to be a year of jubilee, and this is...this is my prayer."

And he starts singing "One" on the most unusual and unique of all imaginable stages, with a giant marble Lincoln behind him. Bono is clean-shaven, white as a sheet, in shirtsleeves, wearing a pair of those oversized glasses of his, without U2, and equipped with only a single guitar, but accompanied by the suave power of a large string orchestra as well as Lanois, who has clearly been summoned to support his voice.

He doesn't sing it well, though "One" is his finest song, his trusted warhorse. Not at all well. He seems tense, constrained, almost excited—Bono, who can't possibly be excited, after having sung with the greatest artists of his time and in all the biggest stadiums on earth and in the most challenging circumstances—such as at the stadium of Sarajevo right after the end of the war in that country, or in the pouring rain at Red Rocks, at the start of his career.

He almost seems to be thinking about something else. He seems preoccupied, actually. He might have just been sick and tired of having to listen to all those old songs and stale speeches, of course, and of having to watch every last second of Spielberg's celebratory short film, and fallen into the booby trap of forcing himself to guess what movies the dozens and dozens of tightly bundled shots were borrowed from, but in the midst of all that happiness, Bono doesn't seem a bit happy to find himself celebrating the great party of the new millennium at the center of the empire that has chosen him as its favorite bard and storyteller.

As he sings, he never smiles, not even once, and in the depths of his bewildered gaze and his hesitant voice we can guess at an uneasiness, perhaps even a malaise that unsettles him and seems on the verge of deflagration from one moment to the next, preventing him from singing his song before the eyes of the world.

Who knows what it is that's bothering him? Is Bono unhappy? Is he depressed? Is he sick? Is he troubled by something that was said or done to him? Did a woman leave him? Did he have too much to drink at the White House? Could he be on drugs? Or else does he feel that he's come to the end of some road and does he believe that the future can offer him nothing better than what he's already had from his astonishing life?

Is Bono thinking about the past or the future?

We'll never know. Maybe he felt the way more or less all of us felt on that fateful day, obliged to celebrate while the lives that we had led until that moment appeared irremediably confined to the past, and we realized that we were on the verge of being catapulted into an immense future about which we knew nothing other than that it was going to mean starting over again from zero in everything, including our very reckoning of the years.

Every so often the camera cuts to Hillary and Chelsea and Bill Clinton watching him as he sings, and while Chelsea seems simply happy and excited, Hillary keeps her gaze fixed on Bono—a faint smile stamped on her immobile face—and moves her head robotically to what she thinks is the ballad's rhythm, thus plainly revealing that she understands neither the lyrics nor the song's inconsolable sweetness. But it's no easy matter to read the vacuous fixity of the president's stare, which manages to appear at once close and distant, both detached and rapt. Still, we can't help but imagine him lost in the contemplation of the last great triumph of his life, because at age fifty-four he's just a little over twelve months short of the end of his second term and the day he bids farewell to the presidency once and for all, on the verge of starting a new life as a relatively youthful retiree, a life that will certainly loom before him as empty and unbearable.

As Bono laboriously manages to work his way to the end of what is certainly one of his most undistinguished performances ever of "One," none of these three protagonists of public life in the last two decades of the twentieth century actually seems to be taking part in the great celebration of the millennium.

Their thoughts run elsewhere, their uneasiness is evident. They're already the perfect image of the future that awaits them. And that awaits us, too.

Edoardo

I WAS BORN ON NOVEMBER 9, 1964, in Prato, an industrial city six miles outside of Florence, and I represent—or perhaps I should say, I once represented—the third generation of textile manufacturers in a family that, before leaping into the great adventure of business, had always lived on little and with little. My great-grandfather Adamo, for instance, was a shoemaker.

Our company had started producing blankets in the 1930s, and after the end of the Second World War, it went on to specialize in fabrics for overcoats and jackets, enjoying a degree of success that endured over the years, mirroring the success achieved by thousands and thousands of small companies just like ours, throughout Italy and throughout Europe.

At our finest moment, we had a total of forty employees who, in total defiance of the idea that they were being exploited by what was so often described to them as the demonic machinations of capitalism, took passionate advantage of that mechanism, showing every day that they cared every bit as much about the company as we did, if not perhaps more, and often teaching us lessons in devotion to their work by the examples they set.

It's a small, true story, 100 percent true, and yet it's only a fragment of the infinitely greater fresco of the history of a people and a nation that emerged from the war, emancipated itself from poverty, and arrived at the end of the millennium after a long and triumphal march.

After the Second World War, in fact, the artisans of Italy gathered the courage needed to give shape to their ambitions, and set out to pursue their dreams of an immense freedom, newly liberated from the yoke of Fascism. By the millions they decided to emerge from the workshops to which their fathers and grandfathers remained proudly confined, and immediately launched themselves into a future that had never before looked so promising. In every Italian city and town hundreds of thousands of small and tiny businesses were born, nearly all of them devoted to manufacturing, which is after all the Italian calling by definition, and incredibly, miraculously, those tiny businesses became successful, in more or less every sector: from typewriters, fabrics, apparel, cars, ceramic tiles, and high-precision machine tools to furniture, shoes, eyeglasses, jewelry, leather goods, motorcycles, and television sets.

It's the Italian provinces as a whole—from Maranello, Prato, Sassuolo, Parma, Busto Arsizio, and Biella to Como, Carpi, Lecco, and Pesaro; from Brescia and Bergamo to San Giuseppe Vesuviano, Martina Franca, Arezzo, Matera, Treviso, Vicenza, Montebelluna, and Santa Croce sull'Arno—that succeeded in shaking off the burden and memory of the foolish autarky to which they had been condemned for twenty years, becoming the locomotive of the Italian economy, suddenly discovering the ability to sell their products throughout Europe and even in America, creating millions of jobs and hauling the nation toward an economic and ethical rebirth that gradually spread to the rest of the country, diffusing through far-flung capillaries into the hearts and minds of those devoutly Catholic people the noblest and most providential dream of capitalism, that exceedingly rare phenomenon that made it something verging on the moral, the fact that it created the conditions whereby a blue-collar worker—if he was capable, if he was determined, if he was courageous—could become the owner of his own company and climb aboard the social elevator that so greatly contributes to a nation's harmony and prosperity, providing a remedy to the injustice of fate that seemed determined to keep earthbound those who had talent but nothing else to their name.

For almost fifty years, most of Italy enjoyed a tumultuous and seemingly unstoppable economic expansion, which continued to offer opportunities to anyone willing to work hard and which spread throughout Italian society a prosperity that might be described as democratic for the way it extended downward instead of remaining concentrated in the hands of just a few, as almost always seemed to happen in the other countries of Europe, allowing Italian women and men to raise exponentially their standard of living.

And so long and so powerful was this growth that it was no longer even perceived as a period or a phase in an economic cycle: it became one of the facts of life, like sunset and springtime.

This was the time of our prosperity, to use Bono's words, and the idea that the future was bound to be better than the present took root in the hearts and minds of an entire people. In those very same days, those disciplines of the soul that are so distant from the work of industrial manufacturing were illuminated by the genius of a flourishing of artistic talents such as had not been since since the time of the Renaissance.

Ah, the Italian art of those years! Lucio Fontana, Alberto Burri, Piero Manzoni, and then Alighiero Boetti, Pino Pascali, Mario Merz, Michelangelo Pistoletto, Jannis Kounellis, Mario Schifano, Gino De Dominicis!

The cinema! Just think of them all hard at work on their sets, practically all at the same time, Roberto Rossellini, Vittorio De Sica, Michelangelo Antonioni, Federico Fellini, Luchino Visconti, Pier Paolo Pasolini, Bernardo Bertolucci, Sergio Leone, Mario Monicelli, directing such actors as Marcello Mastroianni, Sophia Loren, Anna Magnani, Gina Lollobrigida, Virna Lisi, Vittorio Gassman, Monica Vitti, Claudia Cardinale, Silvana Mangano, Gian Maria Volonté, Ugo Tognazzi, Giancarlo Giannini, and Alberto Sordi!

From Milan, industrial design held sway over the world, thanks to the work of Giò Ponti, Bruno Munari, Ettore Sottsass, Gaetano Pesce, Gae Aulenti, the Castiglioni brothers, and Carlo Scarpa, and those same years marked the birth of the great Italian fashion of Emilio Pucci and Gattinoni, Elsa Schiaparelli, Mila Schön, Sorelle Fontana, Gucci, Brioni, Ferragamo, and the forgotten genius Walter Albini, and now here comes Valentino, Giorgio Armani, the Fendi sisters, Versace, Ermenegildo Zegna, Missoni, Gianfranco Ferré, Romeo Gigli, Massimo Osti, not to mention Prada and Dolce & Gabbana...

It was in these years that Italy became the country where life was better than anywhere else on earth, where widely enjoyed prosperity and the beauty of the surroundings were accompanied by the dazzling brilliance of the work of the artists. It isn't easy to explain why all of this should have happened, apparently all at once, in a nation that for centuries had lived jealously clinging to its traditions.

In "Ghostkeeper"—a tangled, formidable, unfinished short story that can be found in the collection *Psalms and Songs*—Malcolm Lowry wrote about "setting some celestial machinery in motion producing events or coincidences," and sometimes I think that this is the perfect explanation to adduce in any attempt to recount the beginning of that benign, invisible, almost miraculous combination of overwhelmingly powerful forces that washed over Italy after the end of the Second World War.

There were many, but we can try to list just a few.

The birth of a freedom and the advent of a democracy that were both wholly new—because in the course of just two years Italy's women and men succeeded in ridding themselves of both Il Duce and the king.

The desire and the need to put behind us once and for all the war and all its tragedies.

The ferment that arrived from other countries and bespoke the advent of an exceedingly fast-moving future, heralded by the ongoing achievements of a friendly technology—almost always American in origin—capable of landing a man on the moon but also of providing a steady, unstanchable flow of mass-market items that cost very little and improved and simplified and even liberated the lives of ordinary people, especially women.

The cascade of rights—starting with the universal right to vote, not sanctioned in Italy until 1946—that sprang directly from liberty and democracy and economic growth and which thundered down upon Italian society, changing it profoundly year after year, making it freer, more open, richer, and more tolerant.

The presence of easily available bank loans that seemed to fall bountifully like manna from heaven upon that army of ambitious businessmen, allowing those who wished to start businesses to do so, and to consume, triggering material dreams and ambitions and enabling practically anyone to buy a washing machine, a car, and even a home.

This wasn't paradise, certainly—if there really is such a thing as paradise—but that young and simple and flourishing nation that at the beginning of every August shut its factories and shops and hastened to kick back on the beaches of the world's most beautiful coastlines and enjoy an entire month off, really might have come close to *the best of all possible worlds*, the one that Doctor Pangloss, the great optimist in Voltaire's *Candide*, continually saw all around him.

Guido

I WAS BORN IN ROME ON AUGUST 27, 1969, and I
remember living through the 1990s as a grand, continuous, thrilling process of acceleration. I didn't have a lira to
my name, and yet everything seemed within reach. There
were days when I could distinctly feel the pressure of a new
world that was testing the boundaries of reality and which
pushed me to give the best of myself in order that I might
be worthy of all the ferment I could sense vibrating around
me. Tomorrow was tumbling down on top of you. In fact,
tomorrow didn't even exist. It was already today.

Like hundreds of other young men and women, in
those years I was a business student on the biggest campus

in Europe, Sapienza University, in Rome, and instead of discouraging me, the predawn alarm and the grueling lines to find a seat for lessons only served to convince me that I was in the right place and doing the right thing.

Every morning, before going in to attend lessons, I'd walk past a plaque upon which was written "The utopia of the weak is the fear of the strong." Those were the words of the economist Ezio Tarantelli, murdered by the Red Brigades in 1985, right there at Sapienza University, and I could feel those words carved into my skin and my heart: I knew it was true, and that it belonged to me, even before I was able to understand it rationally. I really did believe in it—in that dream of the weak who finally win. I had no other choice, for that matter. Because I was one of them.

It was the Internet that helped us to win in that version of ours of an invasion of heaven. Suddenly, thanks to the increasingly fine-grained diffusion of the Internet, there was no longer a physical limit to the possibilities of communication or the circulation of knowledge. In a certain sense, there no longer existed a physical limit to the planet. Everything was within reach, ready to be known and shared, even our dreams.

In fact, our dreams especially, because while until the 1980s dreams had been by and large the result of the deployment of one's personal ambition, the fuel driving one's need to have more because one wanted more, in the nineties the dream expanded and spread until it became a sort of gigantic generational aspiration to seize and make one's own the immense change that was about to over-turn the status quo.

This was a time of technological revolution, and we wanted to be the ones—my contemporaries and I—who were going to write the new rules of that new world that, even as it became immense, was also becoming simpler, since, in order to explore it—and then, as became clear, to command it and control it—all you needed was a computer and a connection to the Web.

Suddenly, we could all sell everything. We were the new artisans, inasmuch as we possessed sophisticated bodies of knowledge, and in order to talk about our jobs, it became necessary to coin new names: knowledge workers, programmers, Web designers, mass communication technicians, bloggers.

We were that very same high-tech service sector that was soon to become global and would be able to invoice the whole world for its expertise because entirely freed from the bonds of full-time, permanent jobs, and therefore eager for virtual autonomy: a brand-new army of individualists capable of working on the global marketplace of the Internet to gather content free of charge and spread it in real time to the eagerly awaiting world, and perhaps coming close to achieving some of old man Marx's ideals—especially when he evoked a world where engineering and technology could free mankind of the burden of hard labor, which would be left to machines and to those tasked with overseeing the most menial, repetitive, automated work.

Set aside for us—and therefore ours by right—was an equally powerful yet completely different productive capacity, infinitely more sophisticated because it was immaterial, based entirely upon language, knowledge, and relationships.

From London, in those years the promised land of young people studying the same things as me, the sirens sang. They flattered me. They wanted me to enroll in the Thames Battalion, as the army of young Italians had been dubbed, an army that had found jobs in major British financial companies and had also managed to avoid wasting the year on military service that was still mandatory in Italy at that time.

I did my best to ignore that siren song. I wanted to stay in Italy and my dream was to do research: to share and set forth in a public university that new body of knowledge that could not be abstracted from the larger and sweeping transformation that was in the air.

Then my girlfriend dumped me. I was earning little or nothing, and I would go on earning little or nothing even if I did manage to become a professor. She told me that she didn't want to spend the rest of her life switching off the hot-water heater in the bathroom until next needed.

And so off I went to London, the capital of global finance, the black hole that sucked in talented young women and men from all around the world and shaped them and changed them forever, overpaying them while they tended, with their unbroken rounds of labor—we got practically no sleep—to the guiding principle of finance, the reason it was created centuries and centuries ago, which is to procure money for those who wish to invest in the real economy.

Finance, in fact, was the fuel that powered the incredible explosion of the Internet. As manufacturing all at once became an antiquated, unprofitable, dirty form of drudge work and the high-tech service sector looked at that point like it was the inevitable future of Western societies, all of the financial operators started investing in technology.

Immense rivers of cash washed over those who wanted to wire the world, connect the planet. Little did it matter that those newly founded companies that boasted hundreds of thousands of contacts online weren't earning a dollar, nor did they have any prospects of earning one in the the future. As long as they were Internet companies, no matter how overstated the claims of their business plans, they were bound to be bought, and so quickly that it created a demented market bubble. Within a few years, that bubble had burst, taking down with it a myriad of those miraculous, evanescent startups — the so-called dot-coms. But the Internet — understood as infrastructure, as an immense welter of cables laid under our sidewalks to bring us a share in the universal information network — had been built. The technological revolution could now begin, and begin it did.

Things went well for me in London. Very well. Finance became a tool with which to gauge my worth and win a place for myself in the world. One day I woke up to discover I was a founding partner in a major asset and investment management company, and I was named the managing director of the London office.

The nineties, in the meantime, were over, and with them the world we had known. Driven by a faith in the future that was undeniable and indestructible because it was borne out with every passing day by reality, we could hardly wait for the year 2000 to arrive, and we merely smiled at the millennium bug, the Y2K scare, the first example of a groundless global fear, an absolute dire certainty trumpeted to the four winds by television networks and radio stations and newspapers in every nation that our civilization was under severe threat from a minor dating problem in the internal clocks of all the computers on earth. It suddenly dawned on us all that those clocks had been programmed with only two places for the year, and therefore no one could say with any certainty whether at the stroke of midnight on December 31, 1999, the world's computers would continue forward through time and enter the year 2000 or lurch backward to the year 1900, upsetting the continuum of events and causing disastrous and absolutely unpredictable effects, such as exploding nuclear power plants and planes falling out of the sky, turning and turning in a spiral of worldwide malfunctions that would send us straight back into the Middle Ages.

We lived on, untroubled and hard at work, in the certainty that nothing bad could happen and that the best was yet to come.

Edoardo

IN THAT PERIOD the daughter of one of our plant workers got married, and for her honeymoon she went to Polynesia. For two weeks.

It seemed like a wonderful thing to me.

Guido

THINGS WERE GOING WELL not only for me and you and all your plant workers, Edo.

That was a time when Italy and the rest of the Western world experienced a carefree optimism and sense of hope for the future that it's downright painful to remember nowadays, and nostalgia has nothing to do with it.

Hearts swollen with the rhetoric that we inhaled with the very air that we breathed, we were all pretty much certain that with the new millennium the planet was finally moving toward the Greater Good, and that the Future would bring more Peace and more Prosperity, all the while nudging mankind toward ever greater Tolerance and Understanding of our fellow humans.

Those capital letters aren't there by accident. Only a few felt any shyness about expressing confidence in the world to come: after fifty years without wars between the great world powers, it seemed only natural to foresee and wish for the birth of ever stronger ties between peoples and nations, and to dream of the construction of increasingly large superstates capable of absorbing conflicts and clashes.

The path seemed marked. History had already come to an end, we were informed, swallowed up by the continuum of the infinite present into which modernity had dissolved, and with it wars and the nationalism that caused them. The continuous global stream of communication brought to us by the Internet would soon eliminate the very concept of distance, allowing us to establish as a common patrimony everything we knew and all that we would learn, thus eliminating both physical and intellectual distances. As walls built of reinforced concrete collapsed, so did the barriers to knowledge, thus freeing the energy created by shared information. We were finally becoming one world and, with the imminent arrival of globalization, world poverty was already in the crosshairs.

We knew that the direction of a country's GDP couldn't actually be the measure of its citizens' welfare, much less of their happiness, but business and finance seemed to be working in harness to create a climate favorable to development throughout the West: the stock exchanges of the world had been rising for years with that slow and steady pace that alone is capable of building and maintaining investors' fortunes, while the economy grew in all directions, unemployment was at historic lows, banks were prospering, the first instances of offshoring were already starting to produce their beneficent effects in those countries in the Far East that we once called underdeveloped and which were now being singled out as the places where growth would be most intensely concentrated.

The only spoilsports were those tens of thousands of activists—for the most part young women and men—who in December 1999, in Seattle, angrily protested the summit meeting of the World Trade Organization, beginning a massive series of mobilizations throughout the West which ought to be given credit for having identified early many of the overarching themes of the antiglobalization movements: opposition to multinationals, demands for the forgiveness of third world debts, the defense of collective interests, pressure for fairer taxation of financial transactions, a new approach toward environmental preservation for the planet at large, support for the struggle to achieve open access and the unfettered sharing of content in defiance of the proprietary boundaries of copyright protection.

While protests raged in Seattle, everything was fine in Italy, and we had no desire to think about the fact that, while the economy might be thriving, the government's balance sheet was plunging.

The value of the national debt, which immediately after the war was stable at 30 percent of the country's gross domestic product, had begun to rise during those years of tumultuous growth, slowly and physiologically, until it had reached 80 percent by the mid-1980s, followed by a sharp uptick that took it to a level of 120 percent in the mid-nineties, receding to 108 percent in 2000—levels that were very different from those found in nearly all other European countries.

This may be an entirely misguided comparison, because a country isn't a company, and it certainly can't be thought of or run like a company, but those are still values that, if applied to a company, would spell its immediate bankruptcy: in fact, they clearly show that its debt is greater than its revenue.

During the growth years, in Germany and in the United States and in Japan and in France and in Great Britain, too—all the great economic powers to which Italy had gradually grown closer in terms of industrial production—what had happened was that private citizens had enriched themselves while the state was growing poorer, though not to the entirely abnormal extent that had occurred here in Italy.

And so, the idea of drawing even closer bonds between the fate of our overindebted country and the fates of European nations far more virtuous than ours—perhaps in the hopes of diluting our unmanageable debt in the larger pool of debt of other, better-managed European countries—met with eager enthusiasm.

In the year 2000, in fact, there was no nation more enthusiastic than Italy about the European Union. An exorbitant percentage of the citizenry said that they were thrilled about *finally making Italy a part of Europe*, embracing without reservations the idea and the project of that union, exulting at the prospect of jettisoning the old Italian lira—whose repeated devaluations had done so much to assist the growth of the country's industry over the years—and adopting the euro, which would become the common currency of a limited number of countries and the undergirding structure of the monetary union that was, however, to be just the first step toward an even tighter and stronger unification: soon it would be followed by fiscal union, a unified banking system, and ultimately political unification.

We were going to become the United States of Europe! A fraternal community of nations newly risen from a terrible war, a war the likes of which must never be seen again! A union of extremely diverse countries, determined in spite of that diversity to live in peace and harmony, and to share the finest of all they had to offer!

The best place on earth, in other words, in the best of all possible worlds. Here he is again, old Doctor Pangloss...

And yet, even taking into account the rhetoric, the euro does become a quantum leap forward into the future. An unprecedented political and financial achievement. An immense, courageous wager designed to give Europe even more development and growth and prosperity.

It doesn't seem to have any weak points. No one, or almost no one, thinks it is a mistake to draw increasingly tight bonds joining a market of half a billion comfortable and evolved consumers, providing them with a single central bank and a single currency strong enough to ensure low interest rates in the individual nations and facilitate easy access to credit, but not so strong as to damage the competitiveness of exports from the single countries.

The euro would become our own dollar, people said, and it would enable Europe to compete on an equal footing with America in every market on earth, especially in those extremely promising Far Eastern markets, China first and foremost.

After all, there was no reason we couldn't become *the best at everything*, people said: with euros in our wallets, Italy had everything to gain, because we could escape the high interest rates of the lira, and the euro would allow our companies to get financing at lower costs, which meant we'd only export even more, earn even more, invest even more, and hire even more. With the euro on our side we'd sweep away the competition — or perhaps I should say we'd continue to sweep away the competition.

There were no doubts about it, in part because along with the single currency we'd also get globalization: an immense word to define an equally immense concept that, in those days, was neither clearly explained nor, most important of all, clearly understood.

Opposition seemed senseless, in any case, since globalization was being described to us as a virtuous and unstoppable historic process bound to bring greater prosperity and justice to everyplace and everyone on earth, a remedy to the consequences of that obscene Western selfishness that had resulted in centuries of worldwide depredations in the wake of our plunder, the firstborn child of colonialism.

In economics, for instance, globalization promised to bring the world the practical achievement of what free-market theory had long called for: the worldwide opening of trade, the elimination of excise duties and tariffs and trade barriers, the introduction of total freedom of capital flows and the movement of services and even of people.

Liberty, in other words.

And with it, money.

Edoardo

SO THIS IS HOW we Italians entered the twenty-first century: with full employment in our factories and full bellies and a gigantic national debt and this two-bit optimism dancing in our head.

There it is at last, the highway to progress, we were informed by a chorus of Nobel laureates and politicians, economists and philosophers and industrialists and commentators, all of them authoritative experts, brought to us over the television and in the newspapers and on the radio and in books and even in movies.

We'll eliminate all impediments to competition so that the free market can work its magic, and we'll all be better off for it: as consumers we'll save lots of money on the television sets and cell phones and videorecorders and computers and tracksuits and camisoles that we buy, and all the other bullshit that we let the Chinese manufacture, because after all there's more than a billion of them in China and they're happy to take bowlsful of rice in payment, while we, as the *Sistema Italia*—the Italian System, a much-vaunted and strictly theoretical concerted effort on the part of manufacturers both large and small, with the support of trade unions and enthusiastically applauded by the workers themselves, widely discussed but never achieved in reality—will be in a perfect position to sell them Italian style.

It was obvious, they told us, in fact, it was *plain as day* that we were just going to mint money with the Chinese: over there, a middle class of genuinely titanic scale was springing into being—hundreds of thousands of people growing wealthier with every passing day, and who were so in love with Italy and its style that they were literally lining up to buy our products.

All that was left for us craftsmen to do was to nod our heads like the little spring-loaded toy dogs you put on car dashboards, and wait.

We weren't going to have to wait long.

On December 11, 2001, China joined the World Trade Organization, the WTO, and on January 1, 2002, euro banknotes went into circulation in Austria, Belgium, Finland, France, Germany, Ireland, Italy, Luxembourg, the Netherlands, Portugal, and Spain.

Impossible to describe what happened next without accepting the help of Malcolm Lowry, who, again in "Ghostkeeper," wonders: "For how could you write a story in which its main symbol was not even reasonably consistent, did not even have consistent ambiguity? Certainly the watch did not seem to mean the same thing consistently. It had started by being a symbol of one thing, and ended up—or rather had not yet ended up—by being a symbol of something else."

It was, in fact, in those few days that the celestial machinery reversed its motion and stopped serving as a metaphor for the rising level of shared growth and prosperity and instead began representing something very different: the onslaught of a terrible economic decline that, in 2001, seemed unthinkable.

Twenty days were all it took for everything to change.

For my family's textile company—which had expanded its traditional production of wool to include a new line of fabrics in linen and cotton and was now proudly supplying the most renowned fashion designers—orders immediately began to become scarce, and then went on declining, and they never did stop declining after that. We didn't receive another order from China.

And it wasn't just happening to my company.

The people of Prato would return from business trips there, all with the same story to tell: the Chinese weren't buying our fabrics, because they'd started manufacturing them themselves for those very same designers who had once been our best customers, but who were now turning their backs on us to save pennies on production costs for overcoats they were selling at three thousand euros apiece, all the while declaring themselves, in newspapers and on TV, to be the proud standard-bearers of Italian style.

It wasn't just happening to the textiles sector.

The whole array of Italian manufacturing—and a substantial share of Western manufacturing as well—slowed almost immediately, and when the requests for temporary layoffs proliferated and then turned into a growing wave of permanent firings and then wholesale bankruptcies, our most brilliant economists denounced us as Luddites, recommending that we try harder to come up with innovative product lines and increase our levels of quality and, as long as we were at it, become the world's finest in our sector. Like Ferrari. Like Giorgio Armani. Like Prada.

They ranted and raved that it was necessary to expand and grow. No more of this conceit that we were craftsmen, enough with the family-run microindustries: the time had come to merge all those little old companies— undistinguished and afraid of their own shadows—into bigger, more modern, *better-structured* companies, and have them run by professional managers, and not by the sons and daughters of the founders. It was time to give up the bad old selfish traditions. That's right! Time to pool our expertise! Time to be done with the idea that individualism is necessarily a good thing!

That's what our betters told us, and we listened, stunned, digging deep into our pockets to find the extra cash to plow back into our companies, trembling as we stammered to ourselves that, after all, our company had given us so much and it was time now to give back to our company—as if that company was a daughter or a mother.

All the while we kept going to China and coming home empty-handed—an immense land that seemed to grow around us during even a short stay, damn it, and it was more than we could fathom how they were able to raze entire quarters of a city in the course of just a few months, replacing them with glass skyscrapers like the ones we'd only ever seen in America.

We who were forced to learn to grit our teeth and fire our employees, though our eyes filled with tears at their disconsolate acknowledgment of the necessity, because they could see for themselves that the world had changed and the company couldn't just go on as if nothing had happened, and before trudging off with their résumés in hand to look for another job, those fired employees would shake hands emotionally, occasionally even throwing their arms around us in a farewell hug.

We who had no idea how to cut costs because it was something we'd never done before, and so, in blind terror of going bankrupt, we cut at random and to excess, so that along with the money and entire divisions, we started losing the youngest and most valuable employees, and with them their energy, ideas, ambitions, and curiosity, and as a result we really did start galloping toward bankruptcy, while we discovered that we were now living in a world we no longer recognized, a world that no longer had any need of us.

And there were those who couldn't stand the shame of finding themselves penniless and unable to pay their debts, and they gradually sold off everything that wasn't bolted down without a word to their families and, while feigning a desperate facade of optimism, they'd plunge into ever darker depths of bleak malaise, convincing themselves they'd never be able to emerge from this abyss, until at last every day that dawned seemed like one more curse and every sunset the bellwether of an endless, sleepless night, as they finally sank into mute despair, spending their afternoons taking long, terrible walks without a thought in their heads except that they couldn't stay home and just watch TV, and then that last Sunday morning when they just couldn't take it anymore and hanged themselves from the highest rafter in their empty industrial shed, leaving a farewell note and an apology to everyone.

They laughed in our faces, we who paid the state more than 60 percent of our profits, and gave our employees buyouts, health insurance, paid holidays, Christmas bonuses, and not one but two extra months' pay a year, and we'd have been happy to pay them even more, because they were the people who helped us keep our companies humming along, if we could only have pried that extra cash loose from the sums we were forced to send to the government in Rome, only to watch them vanish, squandered, down a bottomless pit of waste.

They laughed at us, we who had the most progressive labor market of all time. (We'd finally given up complaining about its byzantine legislation, because it only seemed right that in Europe, in the third millennium, a working relationship should entail the possibility of part time when needed, maternity leave, paternity leave, and personal leaves; that there should be anti-noise regulations to protect the hearing of employees who had to work in buildings where the noise could hit levels of as much as ninety decibels, and a law against workplace mobbing and all other forms of workplace discrimination, and a law against firing without advance notice, and a law ensuring that the disabled had full rights to work.)

They told us yet again that, whether we liked it or not, globalization was an inevitable historical necessity, and that to try to fight back against it would be pointless and even stupid.

They called us backward for wanting to go on living in a little old-fashioned world that no longer existed.

They told us that we were conservatives who were afraid of new things, that we were like the Hobbits of the Shire.

They patiently explained to us that we hadn't understood a thing, and that there was no reason to be afraid of outsourcing because, for every job that was shipped off to China, there would soon be a new and better one created in Italy. Really, that's what they actually told us.

They called us incompetent, we who were the finest craftsmen in the world. Then they turned their backs on us and forgot we'd ever been there in the first place.

Guido

LET ME TELL YOU A STORY.

It's a story about a salamander. I don't remember its scientific name, but even if I did, that would make no difference, nor would it add anything to what I have to say.

It was a rather rare species of salamander, though. That much I clearly remember. I think it lived in Israel. It was endangered, so one fine day—perhaps because of that medieval legend that claimed this little amphibian could miraculously withstand flames—a group of scientists decided to intervene on its behalf and create a protected preserve, to give this salamander a chance to survive and prosper.

In a desert region, therefore, dozens of leafy trees were planted, and the area was watered so that the trees would grow tall and stout. In short order, that unhospitable setting became a sort of oasis for the salamanders, which flocked there in search of a haven, took possession of the site, and quickly began to flourish and multiply.

Not much time passed, however, before the same habitat attracted the attention of a bird in search of a good place to nest: after all, that newly created man-made environment had all the right conditions for this species as well.

Now I *do* remember the bird's name. It's the southern gray shrike, a small bird of prey, about 25 centimeters in length and tipping the scales at just 60 grams. It hunts from the highest branches, plunging down on its prey to catch it unawares. It's also known as the butcher-bird because of its habit of impaling the remains of its victims on thorn branches.

Just see if you can guess what this bird wound up eating.

In a few weeks, not one of those salamanders was left alive. They'd vanished forever from the face of the earth.

This story could be read as an example of the harm that human activity can inflict on animals, even through the well-intentioned act of modifying their habitat, ostensibly for their benefit, and it might even be seen as a warning of the danger of meddling with the rules of nature, a temptation that has already created so many disasters, from mass extinctions to global warming.

But Professor Bruce Robertson, a biologist at Bard College in New York state, puts forth a much more interesting and profound theory. Robertson says that the salamanders have wound up in an "evolutionary trap."

Don't worry if you've never heard of evolutionary traps before. The study of these phenomena is still in its early days, and the term is used for the most part in treatises on ecology and behavioral science to indicate *a grave case of behavioral disadaptation that occurs when, as a result of human intervention, the signals that animals normally use to guide their behavior are uncoupled from the possibilities of survival.*

In simpler terms, it's what happens when, faced by a sudden environmental change caused by man, an animal goes into a tailspin—so to speak—and winds up choosing a behavior that will lead to its death. Even though the salamanders in question hadn't chosen any sort of behavior incompatible with their survival—the evolutionary trap, in fact, was triggered independently of any decision on their part, when a predator was invited to come and settle in their habitat.

There's another story that's even more interesting for the purposes of our book. Because evolutionary traps have other ways of snapping shut, even crueler and more terrible. So listen to this other story.

For thousands of years, a species of sea turtle—the name of which, let me state immediately, I have forgotten, if I ever knew it—undertook a very lengthy oceanic migration to reach a particular tropical beach where it laid its eggs.

When the eggs hatched, the little sea turtles emerged from the sand and headed toward the water, obeying instructions encoded in their genes that commanded them to head toward the starlight and moonlight that reflects off the ocean. It's a perfect, infallible method. It's worked for millennia.

But a few years ago, people discovered the beauty of that tropical beach, and someone built a road along it. Then they put up streetlights along the road, and behind the beachfront road, hotels and bars were built with their brightly lit signs, and so now the newly hatched baby turtles trundled off toward *those* lights, instead of the light of the moon, and they died in their hundreds before anyone noticed and volunteers could hurry out to pluck them up off the road and put them into the water.

This too was an evolutionary trap laid as a result of a change in the environment due to human intervention, but in this case what came into play was the extraordinary phenomenon of an *error in the choice the animal makes*—which is precisely what we're interested in.

In this case, it was precisely the most advanced and evolved trait of the little sea turtles—their extraordinary, seemingly magical ability to get their bearings just minutes after being born, heading toward moonlight and starlight—that, instead of constituting an impressive survival tool, suddenly became harmful and led them to their deaths.

The environment changes and you make the wrong choice, and what condemns you is your own finest quality.

You die because you're better.

Edoardo

CHINA OUGHT TO DECLARE December 11 a national holiday. That's the day, in 2001, when it was admitted to the WTO, the World Trade Organization.

It was a triumphant entrance.

The Chinese were admitted without conditions of any kind.

They weren't even asked to *start* shifting their labor legislation closer to the system of norms, regulations, rights, and social protections achieved by workers in the West after decades and decades of labor organizing and struggles.

They weren't even advised to *begin* reducing pollution from their light and heavy industries, to limit atmospheric carbon dioxide emissions, or to respect international copyright and trademark protections.

They weren't even asked to refrain from using toxic colorants and dyes on products intended for children, such as toys and pajamas.

And most important of all, the Chinese weren't even told to *begin* conceding a semblance of civil rights to their citizens: a crumb—a miserable crumb—of democracy.

Of all the mistakes made by those who were the appointed or elected custodians of the fate of the West, that was without a doubt the worst.

What did they think, that they were going to be able to tame China?

Were they really naive enough to think that the market forces they meant to instill in the Chinese system with the advent of globalization were so powerful that they could even overturn that dictatorship, just as they had the Kremlin? Were they relying on a spontaneous and overwhelming uprising of hundreds of millions of enthusiastic consumers of McDonald's Quarter Pounders and Cokes? Had they seriously forgotten what had happened only a few short years earlier in Tiananmen Square?

Because only in a democratic system, let me say it now, is the citizen guaranteed the freedom of thought and action that allows him to become an individual capable of bringing about the effects of economic theories in society.

You cannot preach free trade and free enterprise and, in the name of that belief, put the fate of the world's manufacturing system into the hands of a dictatorship's subjects: subjects aren't citizens, they're not voters, and most important of all, they aren't free, and therefore they can't behave in accordance with the predictions of free-market economic theories.

They'll obey the laws that the Chinese Communist Party imposes upon them, and certainly not the laws of the market, those hundreds of millions of Chinese workers who maybe, someday, will form a middle class. Their decisions will not be—cannot be—the sort of virtuous free choice that will spontaneously reward the best options offered in terms of quality and price: they'll buy what the Chinese Communist Party allows them to buy.

In the future, scholars may find it hard to believe, I do understand that. Still, this is exactly the way it was that, with foolish and unfounded hopes, the free and rich and advanced Western world—the lands where elected representatives in the legislatures debate, and rightly so, the conditions in which livestock is transported to the slaughterhouse—opened its markets to a dictatorship, without even bothering to demand in exchange the adoption of any of those fundamental human rights that constitute the Western world's history and soul and the basis of its laws—rights that at the same time constitute a substantial part of its companies' operating expenses.

So the dictatorship politely says thank you and then storms into the networks of world trade, seizing for itself total independence and freedom of action, drawing on the theories of free-market capitalism, but only the parts that suit it. With incomparably lower labor costs than its European and American counterparts, and in less time than it takes to say, it seizes a substantial share of the world's manufacturing for itself.

It's the bird of prey that comes to build its nests on the salamanders' territory.

Guido

ITALY IS NOT ALONE in failing to understand. Most of the West stands by idly watching while its manufacturing base is hollowed out and China starts to produce everything that the world consumes, investing the immense trade surplus that immediately begins to accumulate in American treasury bonds.

It's as if, all at once, a new continent had come into being. Rich and growing fast. Self-sufficient. One of the most influential business magazines dubs it *Chinamerica* and provides an illustration of its flag, with the four stars of Beijing's red banner next to the stars and stripes of the American flag.

It's much more than a win-win deal, a pact with advantages for both sides.

It's the winning gambit. The final gambit, perhaps.

The perfect evolutionary trap.

Edoardo

AFTER TAKING THE CHILDREN to school I go into this café I've never set foot in before; I flash a smile at the woman behind the counter and order a cappuccino and two pastries. I take them to a table and sit down.

I drink the cappuccino in small sips and with each sip I try to eat a piece of pastry, which out of an age-old habit I break off with my fingers from the main part of the pastry because I can't stand to see it lopped off by the sharp crescents of my bite.

I watch the people who enter and leave the café, after hastily ordering and drinking an espresso, or topping off the minutes on their cell phone or buying sheafs of bus tickets. I listen as they chat with the barista.

When the cappuccino is finished, I still have more than half of the second pastry left. I eat it slowly, chunk by chunk, and then I start reading the *Gazzetta dello Sport*, from the first page to the last, whereupon I learn the surprising results of the Formula 1 Powerboat Grand Prix Malaysia, which was held in Putrajaya, *on the spectacular course that runs right past the majestic Putra Mosque*. The winner was a forty-year-old Venetian, Fabio Comparato. Then I move on to the *Corriere dello Sport-Stadio*, and I read it, too, from start to finish.

There are no other newspapers, so I glance up and I see the barista looking uncertainly at me. Only for a fleeting instant, though, because she immediately starts wiping down the counter, as if she were afraid I might say something disagreeable to her, because I'd noticed that she'd been looking at me.

I realize that for more than half an hour I've been sitting there, in silence, and so I get up, I pay for that breakfast so different from my usual morning meal—traditionally just an espresso and then I'm off, on the run—and I leave the café.

That's how my first day of unemployment begins. It's nine-thirty on a cloudy Monday in late September 2004, and I have nothing to do.

Two weeks previous, I had sold my family's woolen mill, and in accordance with the terms of the agreement,

I continued working in the company until the evening of
the last Friday to facilitate the transition between the old
and the new owners. Carmine, our warehouse employee,
helped to pack my possessions into a yarn crate, which
we were then able to fit into the trunk of my car. We said
farewell with a brief hug and then I went home.

I don't remember what I did over the weekend,
except to continue to think that it was my fault that we'd
been forced to sell. Everyone told me that wasn't true.
That it was unfair, and even cruel. That it's not my fault,
because keeping a textiles company going in Italy in the
twenty-first century is a task not even remotely compara-
ble to the task of operating one in the 1980s and nineties.
That everything is broken, the whole system, and not just
our company.

I smile, I thank them, but I know there used to be a
company, and now it's gone. I'm the one who sold it, and
this morning I couldn't even bring myself to drive past it.
There used to be a future, and now there is none. I sold
that, too, and for a pittance. Whom should I blame, then?
The mean old world?

I expect I'll go on like this for quite a while. Maybe
for years. Stabbed in the chest by these questions that I
certainly don't know the answer to, defeated, pummeled
by my sense of guilt, diminished, embittered, hollowed
out, incapable of explaining to myself the lack of meaning in everything that is bound to appear before my eyes
every morning—because here, right in front of this café
that I've just left and which I'll certainly never set foot

in again as long as I live, I clearly and fully realize that mornings are going to be the worst moment of the day, with the way they cruelly open out into nothing. My new nothing.

I'll force myself to smile, of course. I'll pretend to be calm and untroubled, relieved, even cheerful, because I don't want anyone to worry about me. I'll learn to conceal the things I really think, and to tell people the exact opposite. A simple and infallible rule of thumb.

In a few days' time, I'll announce that I've finally got my old life back, because I'd never really wanted to run a business in the first place, and it hadn't much suited me anyhow, and who knows if anyone will believe me. Who knows whether, outside of my own family, anyone will even give a damn how I'm doing.

In any case, starting today, depression has become your realm, Edoardo, and you'll visit it every day that God gives you here on earth, cantering down on the white charger of guilt, and unfailingly escorted by the snarling stray dog of your incompetence.

Only poetry will come to your aid, every now and then, and it would be advisable that you memorize what Leopardi wrote in the *Zibaldone*, to give yourself a passing smile from time to time, and comfort yourself with the cowardly thought that, however bad your malaise, someone was once worse off than you are now. *Much* worse off than you.

"Everything is evil," writes the maestro, in fact. "That is to say everything that is, is evil; that each thing that exists is an evil; each thing exists only for an evil end; existence is an evil and made for evil; the end of the universe is evil; the order and the state, the laws, the natural development of the universe are nothing but evil, and they are directed to nothing but evil. There is no other good except nonbeing; there is nothing except what is not; things that are not things: all things are bad."

Who knows for how much longer the buildings, the streets, the cars, and the clouds will seem to you like so many stage props, the world an immense backdrop in a theater where the ridiculous tragedy of a man, and a people, is being staged.

Because you see—*you know*—that you weren't the only one who failed, and that hundreds, and even hundreds of thousands of people have lost their jobs since the new millennium began, in Italy, in Spain, in Portugal, in Greece, and even in France.

These were people who came out of manufacturing, as you did. People who transformed raw materials into products. Small business owners. Craftspeople. Technicians. Factory workers.

Too many, for all of them to have been incompetent.

And soon there were millions of them.

There are millions of people out of work in Europe.

How did that happen? How did it all come to this?

Why did everything that had been going so well suddenly start going so badly, and why hasn't it stopped going badly ever since?

Whose fault is it?

Guido

THERE'S ANOTHER FUNDAMENTAL POEM, Edoardo. William Butler Yeats wrote it, and it's called "The Second Coming."

> Turning and turning in the widening gyre
> The falcon cannot hear the falconer;
> Things fall apart; the centre cannot hold;
> Mere anarchy is loosed upon the world,
> The blood-dimmed tide is loosed, and everywhere
> The ceremony of innocence is drowned;
> The best lack all conviction, while the worst
> Are full of passionate intensity.

Surely some revelation is at hand;
Surely the Second Coming is at hand.
The Second Coming! Hardly are those words out
When a vast image out of *Spiritus Mundi*
Troubles my sight: somewhere in sands of the desert
A shape with lion body and the head of a man,
A gaze blank and pitiless as the sun,
Is moving its slow thighs, while all about it
Reel shadows of the indignant desert birds.
The darkness drops again; but now I know
That twenty centuries of stony sleep
Were vexed to nightmare by a rocking cradle,
And what rough beast, its hour come round at last,
Slouches towards Bethlehem to be born?

Doesn't it strike you as the perfect image of an inexorable evil coming your way? You'll forgive me, I hope, if—for the purposes of this book of ours—I write that that "shape with lion body and the head of a man, / A gaze blank and pitiless as the sun," that "mov[es] its slow thighs, while all about it / Reel shadows of the indignant desert birds" strikes me as a perfect metaphor for debt?

Imagine that rough beast, stalking out of the desert of our attention, in silence, unseen, in the America of 1999, and to be exact, on the twelfth day of the month of November, when a Bill Clinton who was already focusing on the celebration of the Millennium Gala, decided to sign the repeal of the Glass-Steagall Act, the American banking law.

It was a law passed in 1933, after the beginning of the Great Depression, and it made a clear distinction between the possible roles of a bank, which was obliged to choose whether to be a traditional commercial bank (the kind that takes in and safeguards depositors' funds and gives loans and issues mortgages to people and companies) or an investment bank—one of those banks that not only operates on the markets on its own behalf and on behalf of its clients, but also provides assistance and consulting services for large corporations, helping them with all their financial needs: from engineering the structure of derivatives to arranging stock market offerings or capital increases, as well as the creation and management of syndicated loans.

The reason for this separation was the determination of American lawmakers to prevent a repetition of what had just happened—namely, that the failure of a bank should hurt even the smallest depositors, and therefore the real-world economy.

After the repeal of the Glass-Steagall Act, all American banks were allowed not only to issue loans, but also to make capital investments in the same companies. Try to imagine merging a submarine with an airplane: investment banks had limited capital holdings but great skill at financial engineering; commercial banks had the deposits of their customers and the cash flow of their companies' revenue.

Thanks to financial leverage—the mechanism whereby a certain sum is given as collateral in order to receive

PART ONE

another, much greater sum in the form of a loan—*the entire bank holdings of the United States* became subject from one day to the next to collateralization in order to secure a quantity of capital that is difficult to calculate without recourse to celestial mathematics. These are immense, theoretical, imaginary sums, entirely untethered from reality, but they are unleashed on the markets and they start to feed them. We might even say, they start to drug them.

Those sums immediately flow to the American real estate market—the least regulated, least supervised market of them all. The citizens of the United States are told that now anyone, really and truly anyone, can borrow the money to buy a house. It's the democratic dream come true: every American citizen can finally own the house she or he lives in. And since this house, newly purchased, is bound to start increasing in value immediately, why not go back to the bank to borrow more money and then buy another one? Now it's possible. Now you can.

But is it a dream, or the beginning of a nightmare? Can factory workers' daughters have two houses and take a honeymoon in Polynesia?

The fact is that this game goes on for years, and the real estate market continues to soar, until one fine day—unbelievably, considering its size—the bubble bursts.

Crushed by the burden of the titanic debts that it's taken on in the real estate market, Lehman Brothers, one of the largest and most respected American investment banks, goes under on September 15, 2008, triggering a financial crisis whose scale is at once immense and unknowable, since most of that bank's exposure on the real estate market—as well as the exposure of all the major banks in the world, and not just in America—is now expressed in derivative contracts, which is to say, private agreements between investors that work according to algorithms formulated to ensure the greatest possible profits during a growth phase, a phase that they clearly imagined would go on forever. Only the problem is that those same algorithms are capable of creating gigantic losses the minute that the wave of growth stops or is reversed.

Never have we come so close to the end of the system as we know it today.

Because banks can't be allowed to go under.

The cornerstone of capitalism is the protection of private property, and banks are the architrave of that guarantee—the fulcrum and the symbol of the covenant between the depositor and the state. The promise that the money deposited in that bank will always be safe, even if the bank itself goes under.

In a global financial system that is totally interconnected like the one in which we live and work, if one banks fails then others are at risk of failure, and along with them the entire American banking system, and with it, the global banking system, and with *it*, the real economy. It would spell the end of modern capitalism.

Perhaps it would be the end *of everything*.

But Lehman Brothers has gone under, and in order to prevent everything else from collapsing—because there are many American banks with out-of-control debts on their balance sheets, banks that are teetering on the edge, on the verge of going under just as Lehman Brothers did—it becomes necessary to take drastic and urgent measures, and so, with the aim of adding liquidity to the market and preventing further collapses, the Federal Reserve starts printing money. Millions and billions and trillions of dollars. It's an ocean of liquidity, and it washes over the American financial system all at once, and it rescues it. Millions of people lose their homes, of course, but Americans' bank accounts remain intact.

This flood of cash is dubbed quantitative easing (QE), and not only does it rescue the American banks, it also expands into the parched plains of the real economy, and it does a great deal of good. The companies manage to drink from this source, they revive, and they start to see profits again. America, as always, starts up again quickly after its collapse, and two months later it triumphantly elects the first black president in its history, Barack Obama.

Europe, in contrast, finds itself facing the financial crisis of 2008 already weakened by the impact of the consequences of globalization, and it immediately tumbles into a very deep recession.

In Italy bank credit is restricted, it withers, and it grinds to a halt entirely. The crisis in the real economy grows worse, if possible, and even the small companies that had miraculously managed to survive until that moment finally start to go under.

Edoardo

AROUND THAT TIME a friend of mine with a small business told me that the worst moment of his week was always Monday morning, around nine-thirty, when he would get a phone call from the bank director announcing that they'd decided at the head office in Milan to reduce the line of credit for the small print shop that he'd inherited from his father.

He had two employees, this friend of mine, and he really didn't need one of them, but since this other employee was in dire straits himself, my friend had hauled him aboard, tightened his belt, and made do with the small work flow he still could muster. His customers, especially the biggest and most illustrious woolen mills, paid him late when they paid at all.

A devout Christian, goodhearted, generous to a fault, this friend of mine had never argued with the bank director: in part out of respect, in part because he was intimidated, he'd never objected to the three reductions of his line of credit, cuts that had hit him hard and unexpectedly on each of the past three Mondays, but he urgently needed what remained of his line of credit because without it he'd be forced to declare bankruptcy, it would spell the end of his business, so this fourth Monday he screwed up his courage to the sticking point and asked the bank director why he was further reducing his much-needed line of credit.

The bank director said that it wasn't personal, he certainly wouldn't have cut his line of credit if it had been up to him, but unfortunately he had no discretion whatsoever in these matters, which were the sole purview of Milan.

My friend asked how they could know anything about his company, up in Milan, seeing that he had annual revenues of half a million euros, at best.

"The problem is the textile industry."

"But it's not like I work in the textile industry. I don't have a spinning mill or a woolen mill, I have a print shop. I print letterhead stationery, forms, questionnaires…"

"But your company is a small, craft-based company. And small, craft-based companies are at risk."

"What do you mean, at risk? My company's not at risk, Mr. Director. My annual turnover is actually growing, excuse me very much…"

"I don't mean your company in particular. Let's just say that all the small businesses in general *are considered* to be at risk. And after all, you mostly work for textile companies, and the textile industry is considered to be at great risk. They've turned the spotlight on the textile industry, up north in Milan. And anyway, after what happened with Lehman Brothers, we're reducing our exposure..."

"Excuse me, Mr. Director, but I don't even know what Lehman Brothers is. And you know, I have lots of customers who aren't in the textile industry, and they're doing fine."

"Your company is in Prato, though, and according to the bank's algorithm it must necessarily work with the textile industry, therefore it's considered on a par with the textile industry in terms of degree of risk. I'm not in charge of the algorithms."

"I don't even know what an algorithm might be, Mr. Director, but I do know that if you start cutting lines of credit, just when companies are starting to face hard times, you're going to bankrupt us all—"

"Hold on, listen to me..."

"Even a small child would understand it, though, Mr. Director, be reasonable...And if we go out of business, sooner or later so will you."

"Listen. Let me give you a piece of advice, as a friend. If you move your offices from Prato just three or four miles away, say to Sesto Fiorentino, where there is no textile industry, maybe up in Milan they might give you back some of the line of credit you used to have. That way you'd trick the algorithm, you see what I mean?"

Guido

AND THEN IT'S EUROPE itself that starts to creak and sway, thanks to a plot twist so implausible that if you read it in a novel it would make you slam the book shut and throw it against the wall and curse the author and swear never to read anything he wrote ever again.

It's the fall of 2009 and George Papandreou, recently elected prime minister of Greece, goes on television and says that the previous governments have systematically falsified the balance sheets of the state, as far back as the end of the 1990s, to ensure that Greece could show figures that would allow it to join the euro.

The rule requires that every country in the eurozone must have a budget deficit no greater than 3 percent of its gross domestic product, on penalty of the immediate imposition of a series of measures designed to restore that ratio to the percentage required.

We ought to point out that this percentage, this 3 percent, is not based on any scientific point of reference. It's not a value up to which or above which any kind of process in a nation's economy automatically kicks in. It's a percentage that was established arbitrarily. If we lend credence to the reconstructions of events offered later, it was established by some obscure bureaucrat at the beginning of the process of European integration, and inserted into one of those fundamental treaties that govern our lives.

Papandreou announces that that year the ratio of deficit to GDP would not fall within the much discussed 3 percent, but instead is going to reach a level of 12.5 percent, whereupon he immediately requests assistance from Europe. That is to say, he asks for billions of euros.

The most overwhelming crisis in the history of the euro immediately breaks out. Since no individual country in the European Union has the power of seigniorage—that is, the right to print money—it looks dangerously likely that Greece and no one else but Greece is going to have to be responsible for guaranteeing the Greek debt—certainly not Europe, which doesn't even want to hear about printing money to pay off Athens's debts.

The markets and the credit rating agencies suddenly seem to discover the implicit weakness of a system that uses a single currency but is composed of twenty different countries—each with its own government, each with its own budget, each with its own deficit-to-GDP ratio, its own economic and tax policies—and they feel encouraged to bet on the likelihood, heretofore inconceivable, that a sovereign state, even though it's a member of both the European Union and the euro might well lose access to the credit markets and therefore become incapable of meeting its obligations, just like any ordinary company.

Because modern states depend on the constant refinancing of their debt. Every month they issue bonds that are purchased by investors—treasury bills—and they use the proceeds from these issues to pay for schools, their citizens' pensions, government services, and the salaries of government employees.

Without that money—without, that is, access to the market—the state will sooner or later be forced to default.

Edoardo

What do you mean, default?

A European country? How can a European country default? Don't we have the European Union backing us up?

What's happening, exactly, anyway? Is it true that pensions and government salaries aren't being paid anymore? And doctors? And hospitals? What's going to happen to the hospitals, are they all going to be shut down and the patients turned away? What about the schools? What about government day care centers?

Are there no longer policemen and Carabinieri patrolling the streets?

And what about electricity, what about running water, what becomes of them?

Will the courts remain open? Who'll collect the garbage? What about the buses, will they keep running? And the trains?

What about churches? Are the churches going to stay open, if someone wants to go and pray?

Guido

THEY SAY THAT FINANCE is like a big dark room, and
that every once in a while someone turns on a flashlight
and aims the beam into a corner. Then everyone realizes
what's in that corner and how important it is, and they all
start to write about it in the pages of the leading world
newspapers and magazines and they don't stop until they
finally come to a general consensus about what needs to
be done.

Then they act.

Now the beam of light is focused on the national debt
of the countries of Europe. Yeats's rough beast has finally
slouched its way to Bethlehem, and this is the moment

when the dream of Europe's founding fathers is finally shattered: when the chance of the monetary union actually breaking apart stops being a hypothesis and takes life, incarnated in a fairly obscure indicator, which until that moment had remained largely stable and was of interest primarily to the scholars of theoretical finance. That indicator is the spread, that is, the difference between interest rates in the securities issued by the hegemonic country, which is to say, Germany, and interest rates on the securities issued by the other European countries.

The spread immediately becomes the ideal instrument for measuring the distance between dream and reality: it's the perfect image, measurable every day in all the stock markets of the world, of the inefficiency of what was in theory supposed to be a single monetary system, composed of countries whose rates of interest were, if not identical, at least very close.

The fluctuations of the spread will be the basis from now on for the value that the market will assign to the sustainability of an individual nation's debts. Or, to put it in simpler terms, the spread will take the temperature of Europe's fever. And that temperature immediately starts to rise.

It's the shattering of a dogma. What had remained in hibernation for years suddenly comes to its senses, and in finance there's nothing more dangerous than something that never moves, because then when it finally does...

Financial operators around the world simultaneously start issuing sell orders for Greek treasury bonds and buy orders for German treasury bonds, which causes the spread to skyrocket and stoke further fears in the markets and among politicians. Everyone is convinced they're about to see Greece drop out of the euro. Perhaps, even, the collapse of the euro itself.

This is the beginning of a crisis that unfolds in pitch darkness, without prospects of any immediate solution and potentially with no way out, because none of the treaties prescribes any mechanism for an exit from the monetary union, which means no one can say what might happen if the situation were to continue to deteriorate.

Incredible as it may seem, a European confederation with a monetary union of no fewer than sixteen countries, as varied as can be, ranging from France to Slovakia, from Holland to Cyprus, never even thought of creating a mechanism to defend the common currency in case of a financial crisis in one of the member states.

We're in uncharted territory now. At these levels of the spread, the Greeks can neither remain in the euro nor exit it.

In the meantime, the Greeks lose access to the markets, because the credit rating agencies wake up and unanimously decree that Greece is on the brink of default, and no one wants to lend the country money anymore.

For that matter, after Papandreou's declaration, the emperor has no clothes.

How can there fail to be an enormous difference between the yield and the value of a German Bund and a Greek bond? How is it even conceivable that Berlin and

Athens are together, in the same Europe, using the same currency? What's more, and above all, how could it be that for twelve long years, no one—neither the European Union, nor the great newspapers, nor the banks (especially the French and German banks), which had even lent enormous sums of money to Athens, nor the credit rating agencies, *no one*—had noticed that the Greek balance sheets had been falsified?

In that case, could the balance sheets of other European countries have been falsified, too? Like, say, the balance sheets of Spain and Italy? And what should we think, then, about the balance sheets of their banks, jam-full of government securities as they are? And what are we to think about the balance sheets of *all* the European banks? Could it be that they're all perfectly sound? What about the British and the Irish banks that plunged so deeply into the American real estate market and are now stuffed to the gills with derivatives? And the Italian and Spanish banks that wrote down charges for the bankruptcies of hundreds of thousands of manufacturing companies?

Whom are we supposed to believe? Or actually, whom can we believe anymore?

Edoardo

THE BEST COMMENT on this whole affair comes unexpectedly, a gift out of the blue, from Roberto Benigni. A journalist asked him what he thought of the Greek debt, and this is more or less what he said, if I remember correctly.

"What? You say Greece is in debt to us? What, is that supposed to be a joke? Have we all lost our minds? Let's hurry over to apologize, to our Greek brothers and our Greek sisters! If anyone is in debt, it's we who are in debt to Greece for everything we hold dearest, everything that has made us what and who we are: art and democracy and beauty and philosophy! And that's a debt to Greece we'll never be able to repay. Never, not till the end of all time! Come on, tell them right away that we were only kidding, otherwise they'll start to worry!"

Guido

IT'S PROBABLY A GOOD IDEA to explain, at this point, that I don't fit into this disastrous panorama, this unstoppable decline, this obscene decay. Maybe I was good at my job, and certainly I was on the winning side, but the establishment in the world of this globalization that tore entire economies limb from limb—including the economy of my own country—took place more or less in parallel with the growth of my career as a money manager.

I only ever benefited from globalization, and the collapse of Lehman Brothers—like every other crisis, for that matter—proved to be, in hindsight, a formidable opportunity for people in my line of work: both for short-term speculators and those with a longer-term objective. The quickest way to make big profits is with market volatility. You can earn big on collapses and on the recoveries that follow.

The best performances in my life as a money manager came from investing in stock markets around the world: investing in companies, or against them. I've always preferred to invest in a company—to buy its shares and watch them rise, pleased that I was proven right to invest in it, and delighted at the yield from the profitable shares, and then happy to sell at the right moment—but I never asked myself whether it was right or wrong to invest *against* a company.

I've done it, at times. It's part of the work I do. It's a counterintuitive mechanism that has always had a certain allure for me, ever since I was a kid. In fact, the way it works is you *short* the shares of a company—meaning you sell them without owning them—in the expectation of a future drop in shares that will allow you to buy those shares later at a lower price, when you complete the transaction.

Companies can go bankrupt, and there are companies that deserve to, they're so badly run. Sometimes it's good for everyone for a company to go under, because its decline and prolonged death throes only poison the wells of the market it's operating in, preventing the foundation of new and better companies.

An entire market sector can even disappear if, for instance, a certain technology or the passage of new laws makes it obsolete. But the market itself always survives. It changes. It regenerates. And if the state is able to amortize the social costs over the short term, it is the market itself, over the long term, that remedies the loss of jobs in the larger system, rehiring the men and women who once worked in the now bankrupt companies, so that they now work in new and better companies. Sometimes I think that bankruptcies are antibodies at work in the healthy functioning of the market's larger body.

Now, however, I found myself forced to invest against a *country*—a free state in that Europe I had always believed in, and which had been one of the bastions of my education, both personal and professional. This time it wasn't the fate of a company that was being called into question, but the destiny of millions of people, Europeans like me, that my colleagues from all over the world and I were putting at risk. Because, if Greece went under, its eleven million citizens couldn't just shrug and abandon it, they couldn't just go and live and work somewhere else.

I realized that the role I was playing had changed. I had stopped being an impartial investor, interested only and exclusively in earning a legitimate profit for my clients, and I had become a sort of subterranean Greek legislator.

That's right, because it was our selling—my own and the selling that my colleagues around the world did—that pushed up the spread and terrorized Europe and forced the Athens government to weigh in repeatedly on the deficit with sudden and draconian measures, approved in the middle of the night by a terrified Greek Parliament while Syntagma Square was besieged by thousands of demonstrators and television crews from every corner of the planet: the Greeks were seeing their income taxes and value-added tax (VAT) hiked at the same time that their pensions and salaries were being cut. Thousands of people were losing their jobs from one day to the next.

To make a concerted and forceful effort to sell a country's debt until you bring it to its knees and succeed in influencing the laws it makes, means becoming a political actor in that country, unelected but immensely powerful. It means undercutting the democracy of that country, and therefore of all of Europe, weakening it until it becomes little more than a shadow of its former self, and then vanishes entirely.

Papandreou was no longer governing Greece. It was me and people like me. If we didn't think a reform was sufficient, we'd intensify the pressure by selling, and we'd force the government in Athens to replace that reform with a harsher one. And no matter how harsh the reforms became, they were never harsh enough to satisfy us. It was never enough, and always too late.

I didn't like impoverishing the Greeks at all. I did it, that's true. Because I had to. I owed it to my clients: I owed it to the fiduciary mandate they'd given me, which required me to ensure they profited. If for any reason I had stopped doing so, someone else would have taken my place. And so, as I sold in order to protect the assets of my clients from the collapse of a country, I kept telling myself that the fault wasn't mine, that I was merely doing my job.

But I couldn't stop watching the images on the television news. The strikes. The constant demonstrations in the streets. The young men in black hoodies who'd start throwing rocks at the police as soon as night fell. The Molotov cocktails. The riot cops with their shields. The unfailingly tense faces of the journalists and their interview subjects. The icy glares of the Nazis of Golden Dawn.

It became hard to sleep at night, and rare that I did. What was stirring my anxiety was not just the economic collapse of Greece. I kept wondering what would become of the other heavily indebted European nations. What would become of Ireland and Portugal. Spain. What would become of Italy.

But it was no longer possible to stop. It was the whole system that threatened to collapse, and no one wanted to be buried beneath the rubble. And so, to cover the risks linked to an implosion of Greek public debt, I started buying CDS's on Greece.

A CDS, which is an abbreviation for Credit Default Swap, is a financial contract that can be used to insure against the bankruptcy of a company—or in this case, the default of a country—that has issued securities: the higher the risk of bankruptcy or default, the higher the value of the CDS. It's a financial derivative, officially quoted and regularly traded, but it's very, very volatile. You should only use them with extreme caution.

Because they are not keyed to any economic benchmark, but are simply a measurement of market consensus about the likelihood that a future event may take place, they can have extreme swings in value. Just to give you an idea, a CDS on Greece was quoted at 4 in July 2007, but it actually soared to 25,400 at the peak of the crisis, when we were all betting—another verb would technically be inaccurate to use—on the collapse of the euro system. Around that time, though, it wasn't so risky to double down on CDS's: Athens wasn't going to be able to extricate itself without help from the quicksand bog it had wandered into, while the rest of Europe simply looked on and did nothing...

Soon, though, the CDS's weren't enough, and I decided to go ahead and sell all the Greek securities I still had in my portfolio. That triggered the collateral thought that led me to wonder what country would next be in the market's spotlight, so I started selling the securities of all the other overleveraged countries that I had in my portfolio. Suddenly, they all started to look much riskier than the market considered them. And so did the treasury bills, naturally.

Then the message began to spread that Athens couldn't fail because its creditors—especially those French and German banks that had grabbed as many Greek government bonds as they could in the past, attracted by the high yields and absence of risk they'd enjoyed until just a few weeks ago—wouldn't be able to afford those immense write-offs.

At the same time, of course, Greece couldn't be saved entirely, because in the eyes of German voters, a European bailout would have constituted a dangerous violation of

the rules, and an encouragement to overindebted countries to go ahead and act the same way, and so, after weeks
of passion, a compromise solution was adopted: one that
was best for the powerful and worst for the weak.

Europe and the International Monetary Fund wound
up issuing a bailout loan of 110 billion euros that, while
on the one hand it gave Athens some oxygen, on the
other hand it imposed further, very strict austerity measures. Too strict for a nation that was already on its knees.
It was tantamount to demanding that Greece pull itself
out of the mire by its own hair, as Baron Münchhausen
claimed to have done.

It was this approach that fed the *contagion narrative*.
If Greece is patient zero, the patient in which the virus
manifested itself for the first time and with the greatest
virulence, then it would be a good idea to take the temperature of other patients as well, to see if they too show
signs of fever, and to judge from the constant rise of the
spread between their securities and German securities, it
looked like Portugal, Ireland, and Spain were also infected.

The problems afflicting these three countries *worried the markets*: that, comically enough, was one of the
phrases most widely used by financial commentators, as
if the people who were worried about the debts of these
nations were only us, the ones selling their CDS's and
securities, rather than the citizens of Lisbon, Dublin, and
Madrid, who were spending their days in front of their
television sets, waiting for good news that never seemed
to arrive.

Immediately after them, of course, it was Italy's turn: Italy, the most heavily indebted country of them all. For that matter Italy had been under medical observation, so to speak, for months now, from the day that Papandreou went on TV to empty the bag of the Greek government's lies. Even though the size of our economy and of our debt is so vast that we're classified as too big to fail, the spread between Italian treasury bills and their German counterparts started to climb. Lehman Brothers, too, after all, had been too big to fail.

They put us all in the same group, and we became Europe's problem. Based on our initials, they started calling us the PIIGS. Portugal, Ireland, Italy, Greece, and Spain.

So now we were pigs.

Edoardo

IT MADE ME FURIOUS, being part of the PIIGS.

I couldn't bring myself to joke about it, take it as something funny. Because it wasn't funny. It was a humiliation. Every time that I heard someone say it on TV, that damned word, I'd change the channel. I was furious. First they take away our manufacturing, our only possession, and then they make fun of us because we're struggling.

The bad guys, the ones who took it away from us, were the Europeans of the north.

Those chilly, wealthy nations that own Europe and set the editorial line for newspapers and television newscasts and no longer do any manufacturing of their own and can therefore blithely sign the treaties that sent all the business to China, because their own citizens live off services and trade and imports.

Those chilly, wealthy nations that have always dictated the conditions for everything that Brussels is going to approve, and have always rejected Italy's timid proposals that we adopt a European system for labeling of origins of all goods, so that a citizen can easily see where the products she buys were made (because that's not the way it is now—it seems worthy of pointing out—Europeans don't know where the things they buy were made, while in America that labeling system has been mandatory for decades).

Those chilly, wealthy nations that want you to continue buying products made in China because it is their multinationals that have them manufactured there, though they'd prefer you not to know it, and so they have their running dogs in coat and tie defend the ridiculous notion that such labeling of place of origin would somehow *distort free competition*, instead of simply providing consumers with an extra piece of information and the opportunity to choose whether or not to purchase a Chinese-made product.

These are the things I thought and said and wrote, filled with a ferocious rage that for the first time in my life I felt I could truly share with millions of other people: it's their fault that we've lost everything, that I've lost everything. It's their fault, them and those incompetents who ran our government at the end of the millennium, those geniuses who were told, "You'll lose millions of jobs. Sign here," and with a smile on their faces, they signed.

Although I hated seeing Italy disrespected in that way, I was absolutely *not* sorry to see my country lumped together with the other Mediterranean nations. We're cut from the same cloth, we and the Spanish and the Portuguese and the Greeks: fellow peoples, children of a shared culture that dominated the world for hundreds of years, people accustomed to living amidst beauty, surrounded by art, basking in bright, warm sunlight, accustomed to eating and drinking the best of what this planet has to offer.

Ireland didn't particularly fit into this picture, especially because its financial crisis had more to do with banks, and that country's economy ran on a completely different basis from ours, but I was pleased to have the company of the Irish in our little group of unfortunate countries. They're likable people, I told myself, related to fairies and leprechauns, and we've never fought with them either. Plus they know how to write and compose poetry and paint and act, because Ireland has been the birthplace of such great masters as Beckett, Joyce, Wilde, Yeats, Stoker, Swift, the artist Francis Bacon, and even Daniel Day-Lewis. They may drink that awful warm beer of theirs instead of wine, but that can be overlooked.

In other words, Italy had been absolved, and I'd been absolved with her. It hadn't been our fault, it was someone else's fault. The Germans and the politicians. They'd tricked us. They'd stolen our work and our prosperity and our future, ours and our daughters' and our sons'. They were all bastards, full stop.

Then one day, my father, now in his early eighties, phoned me.

"Good morning, son, I just read an article in *Il Sole-24 Ore* where it says that we're in terrible shape, that German manufacturing is going great guns, in fact it's never done as well as it's doing now. But what exactly is it that they manufacture? Do you happen to know? That is, have they changed what they produce or are they still making what they've always made?"

"They make what they always have, Dad. Cars, plastics, chemicals, pharmaceuticals, industrial machinery, and rubber. The usual German things…"

"Ah, sure…I remember them, you know, those immense plants along the highways, those gigantic smokestacks three hundred and more feet tall that we always saw when we went up there to sell them loden fabric…"

"So do I, Dad. We were there together."

"Yes, but now I'm asking you about it because while we're in a severe downturn, it would seem that they're doing just fine. Their exports are going great guns. Is that what you're hearing?"

"Yes, certainly. They're doing well. It's true."

"They're even exporting to China, according to this article that was in *Il Sole-24 Ore.*"

"Yes, that sounds right."

"So how do they do it?"

My father had agreed to the sale of the family company, which he had inherited from his grandfather while it was still small and in parlous condition. Over the years he had made it into a successful powerhouse, but he no longer thought that textiles had a future. Since he stopped working, he's become a much happier person. He's finally been able to devote himself to my mother, to reading, and to Beethoven. He's even become religious. He's turned into a fervent Christian. He attends Mass. He prays. Sometimes he sings in church. Every so often he even tries to convert me.

"Huh, Edo, how do they do it? How come they can do it and we can't?"

I didn't know the answer. I mumbled something about certain European tariffs that were left in place to protect special, very German sectors such as chemicals and steel-making, but that was no answer, and he knew it.

"Do a little research on the Internet for your old father, please. Find out how they're doing it. I'd be interested in finding out…"

I promised I'd look into it, and we said goodbye. But I couldn't get that question out of my mind. How did the Germans do it? It didn't take me long to discover the existence of the Fraunhofer Society, a public-private network of applied research laboratories with an annual budget of 2.1 billion euros, 30 percent of which is financed by the German government, while the rest comes from contracts with private manufacturers and state-financed research projects.

The Fraunhofer Society began its activity in 1954, when it established its first research institute. Today there are sixty-nine of them, scattered the length and breadth of Germany, and they employ *twenty-four thousand scientists*.

These sixty-nine institutes don't do theoretical research. They work exclusively on translating into industrial innovation the results of the most advanced research, and it is their constant collaboration with small and medium-sized companies—which apparently continue even now to be the engine of the German economic system—that gives those companies the competitive edge that allows them to prosper while still manufacturing at home, exporting high-priced technological products that become impossible to make elsewhere.

While we relied upon the uncontrolled and irreproducible talents of our entrepreneurs and basked in all sorts of nonsense about our thousand-year-old culture and the art and beauty of the most beautiful country on earth, and how those qualities in some miraculous way would be instilled in our products, allowing us to go on selling them forever and everywhere, Germany was building a massive and powerful research system that studied and developed practically everything (from algorithms to photonics, from measuring systems to logistics and lasers and industrial mathematics and nanotechnologies and solid-state physics and immunology), but it focused in particular on projects that might have immediate industrial applications for German companies.

In this system built for the sharing of patented and protected technologies it becomes absolutely fundamental that the manufacturing of the product is done in Germany because, as they insist at the Fraunhofer Society, *we can only continue to pursue and attain true innovation if we're doing the manufacturing.*

So manufacturing in Europe isn't finished, after all.

It's just *our* manufacturing that's finished: our poor and brilliant and ancient and anarchistic and completely disorganized manufacturing, ignored by the state, produced with machinery that was purchased by our fathers, using methods that we'd learned from our grandfathers.

Crushed, I went to see my dad and tell him about it.

He listened carefully, without a word. He just asked me to repeat the number of researchers working for the Fraunhofer Society: twenty-four thousand. When I was done, he smiled bitterly and thanked me.

Then he turned to look out the window, into the empty air.

Guido

ON OCTOBER 19, 2010, Angela Merkel and Nicolas Sarkozy meet at Deauville, an elegant little coastal city in Normandy, and are photographed in bliss and harmony as they walk along the beachfront.

Both the same height, both dramatically badly dressed, they stroll and gesticulate, surrounded by bodyguards and functionaries, photographers and TV cameramen, against the backdrop of a broad, empty beach.

Edoardo

FOR THE FRENCH, Deauville is a legendary beach.

Coco Chanel used to go for strolls on that beach. And that's where Anouk Aimée and Jean-Louis Trintignant fell in love, in Claude Lelouch's *A Man and a Woman*.

Guido

THE INTENTIONS OF *this man* and *this woman*, however, are far less romantic. They've just made decisions they'll soon bitterly regret, and on the eve of a European summit conference, they want to display unity of intention of the two most important nations about how to confront the Greek financial crisis and all the other crises that might follow.

They've just decided—and they'll have the statement included in the official press release issued at the end of the European summit—that "the sovereign debt of a European nation can be restructured."

Behind the chilly complexity of the language of official statements an enormous new development lies concealed, from Deauville forward: *the sovereign debt of a European nation can no longer be considered inviolable.* That is, the bonds already issued by any given European country might not be reimbursed entirely, in the future.

It's a short sentence that follows, however, that really shakes to the foundations the very idea that investing in a treasury bill from a country in the eurozone can continue to be a substantially risk-free activity.

It states in the official communiqué that "the involvement of the private sector will be imperative in any future bailout."

In other words, in practical terms, what Merkel and Sarkozy are telling us is this:

"Ladies and gentlemen, those of you who bought treasury bills convinced that you were perfectly safe because Italy is in Europe, well, please be aware from this day forward that you aren't safe anymore. There is no European guarantee that your capital is going to be returned to you, intact, when the bonds reach maturity. Your debts are yours and yours alone. Practically speaking, you're in the same condition as the Greeks.

In Italy, in that period, very few worried about it.

Perhaps very few understood.

Edoardo

WE KNOW ABOUT IT, about our national debt, of course we do.

People have been saying over and over again for decades that it's very high and that we need to do something, because there's a risk it might become unserviceable, untenable, but by now it's become too big to really worry about it.

As we write now, it's *2.25 trillion* euros: a quantity of money so immense that it transcends human understanding and becomes an absolute and indubitable entity, invisible and yet certain, as distant as we hope our own deaths to be.

We no longer feel as if it's ours, and we can never repay it. There are already people clamoring in the streets that we ought to stop bankrupting the country just trying to service the interest on it.

It's the cost of the life we've been living, we tell ourselves. Of the country that we built. Of the rights that we won for ourselves. Of the incompetence and corruption of those who governed us in the 1980s—when that debt exploded, damn it, almost doubling over the course of fifteen years.

But now that we have factories closing and people demonstrating in the streets, should we worry about a national debt of 2.25 trillion euros? It would be like worrying about the fact that in several billion years the sun is going to nova and then burn out.

And so we pay no attention to it.

We pretend nothing's happening.

All of us. A whole country.

It's the most colossal case of collective denial in history.

Guido

A LITTLE OVER A YEAR LATER, on October 23, 2011, there's a European summit conference in Brussels, and at the end of the conference Merkel and Sarkozy hold a joint press conference.

"What did you say to Signor Berlusconi?" a female journalist asks Angela Merkel. "Did he promise any commitments to new reforms in Italy? Are you reassured?"

During the question, Sarkozy starts to smile. Merkel mantains a serious expression until the end of the question and then, instead of answering, she turns to look at Sarkozy, sees him smiling, and she starts smiling too.

It's a pause that's so perfect, it seems rehearsed, and the world's press, assembled there, breaks out laughing.

Edoardo

THAT'S RIGHT, because the leader in charge of Italy's government is Silvio Berlusconi, president of the A.C. Milan soccer club who, in 1994, announced his candidacy to the Italian people with a television message recorded in the living room of his home.

Sitting at an uncluttered desk, upon which there were only a couple of pieces of glass bric-a-brac and a stack of papers, to convey the idea that he's just been interrupted while hard at work; clearly visible behind him is a bookcase, where several silver-framed family photographs enjoy pride of place, along with an abstract microsculpture, and a dozen or so books that fail to fill the shelves. They looked as if they'd just been put away hastily, unread, between one business phone call and another. He said:

> Our left-wing parties claim that they've changed. They say that they've become free-market democrats, but that's not true! Their people remain the same, as do their mindsets, their culture, their deepest underlying convictions, and their behavior. They don't believe in the markets. They don't believe in private enterprise. They don't believe in profits. They don't believe in individuals. They don't believe that the world can become a better place through the free contributions of a great many people, each different from the others. They haven't changed. Listen to them speak. Watch their television news broadcasts, paid for with government money. Read their press. They no longer believe in anything.

He added: "We believe in the individual, the family, the company, competition, development, efficiency, free markets, and we believe in solidarity, the daughter of justice and liberty."

He smiled only once, as he came to the end of that radically new statement, after the grand finale: "I say to you all that we can achieve a great dream, the dream of an Italy that is more just, more generous to those who are in need, more prosperous and peaceful, more modern and better run, an Italy that plays an active role in Europe and the world. I tell you that we can, that we must work together to build—for ourselves and our children—a new Italian miracle!"

Silvio Berlusconi, who a few months later won the election hands down and triumphantly entered Palazzo Chigi, the Italian White House, holding himself up as a paragon of virtue and luring the Italians into a simple and perfect dream, promising to be at once the creator and the custodian of that dream, only to tender his resignation eight months later in the wake of an investigation by the Milan prosecuting attorneys' office into his corporate holdings.

Silvio Berlusconi, who didn't know how to govern a country and never did learn how, and who would have done everybody else and even himself a favor by just tending to the business of his media empire, and who instead was forced to spend every day of his time as prime minister of Italy working on his defense in the dozens and dozens of trials to which the Italian judiciary decided to subject him once he chose to enter politics, and yet who did do one great thing, on Easter Sunday of 1997, when he went down to Brindisi to visit with the survivors of the first great tragedy of illegal immigration.

Perhaps you don't remember. What had happened was that a boat, packed to the gunwales with immigrants—back then they were still referred to as illegals—had been halted in the waters off the coast of Puglia by an Italian navy warship and in the great veering and crashing of the embargo operations—in that period Italy under the administration of Romano Prodi had adopted the deplorable policy of turning back would-be immigrants on the high seas—that boat had been rammed. It went down in the blink of an eye. Eighty-six people drowned. All of them Albanians.

Berlusconi boarded a plane and flew down to meet the survivors and then he appeared in front of the television news cameras with puffy eyes and a broken voice.

"I wish that all Italians could have met the people I just met, people who've lost three children, who've lost their wife, who had hoped to come here to find a free, democratic country, where they could work, where they could show what they could achieve. You know, these are things that we can't let happen in this country of ours..."

Then he turned to the journalists and excused himself, so deeply moved that he was on the verge of tears, with those few strands of hair combed back and wearing a navy blue crewneck sweater, underneath which you could just spot the collar of a sky-blue shirt, suddenly short and hunched over and awkward, helpless and diminished as only powerful men are able to seem when they come face-to-face with a power so immensely superior to their own, but certainly sincere, because he had nothing to gain politically—if anything, he had everything to lose—by tearing up in public over the deaths of eighty-six Albanians.

Berlusconi wept, profoundly human and overwhelmed by emotion in a way we'd never see again, and he betrayed no shame, he was utterly indifferent to the fact that his tears and his words would upset his voters who in general, and in part, are people who—let's just say—are less attentive to the more awful realities of immigration.

As prime minister, Silvio Berlusconi churned out spectacular gaffes by the dozen, and you may well have seen many of them on TV.

The time that he announced that he had warded off the *world war that was about to break out* over the border conflicts between Georgia and Russia, by persuading Obama and Putin to make peace.

The time at Baden-Baden that he kept Merkel and all the European heads of state waiting because he was talking on the phone with someone, and then tried to make amends by explaining that he was deep in conversation with Putin.

The time in October 2010 when, right in the midst of the economic meltdown, he announced during a speech that the Italian left wing's insistence on wanting to kick him out of office and send him home created a certain uneasiness in his mind, "because seeing that I own twenty homes, I'm not sure which of them I'd have to go to."

The time that he hid behind a monument and called out peekaboo to Angela Merkel. The time that he held up two fingers, making devil's horns behind the head of a Spanish cabinet minister in the commemorative group photo for a European summit meeting. The time that he called out loudly at Buckingham Palace (*Mr. Obamaaaa!*) and got a scolding from the queen. The time that he explained that Obama, once again, was a handsome, suntanned young man. The time that, in a fateful news conference, he declared that " 'Gogol' can do a great deal to help Italian companies," and while Mubarak listened to him, impassive, with the face of a stone head from Easter Island, he went on, ranting about "special courses in 'Gogol' to be taught to Italy's small and medium-sized businesses, allowing them to conquer the world's markets."

That was the press conference that was followed by the lunch at which Berlusconi claimed he asked Mubarak if he really did have a young and beautiful niece who was living a somewhat bohemian lifestyle in Italy.

That's right, because while Merkel and Sarkozy were tittering about him in public, Berlusconi had already gotten himself neck-deep in trouble with that investigation of "fancy dinners" that was going to make a fool of him before the rest of the world. He'd already put in a phone call to Milan's police headquarters to alert the functionaries there that Karima El Mahroug, aka Ruby Rubacuori—an underage young woman who'd just been arrested on suspicions of theft and without any legal ID—"was the niece of Hosni Mubarak" and should therefore be released immediately to prevent an international diplomatic incident. He had already arranged for his parliamentary majority to vote in favor of a resolution stating that, inasmuch as the prime minister of Italy actually believed, when he made that phone call to police headquarters to demand Ruby's immediate release, that the young woman was the niece of the president of the Arab Republic of Egypt, he had therefore been acting within the proper domain of his official duties, and could not therefore be prosecuted by the magistrates in Milan.

Silvio Berlusconi who, not even four months after those leaders tittered at him, would be indicted for bribery and prostitution with a minor, and all the television networks in the world would broadcast footage of him leaving one of his mansions in a black limousine with a furrowed brow, accompanied by his own utter ruin and pursued by journalists and suspicions and unanswered questions, branded for all time by the *bunga bunga*, the horrendous nonsense sounds borrowed from some dirty joke or other, one of those old groaners he loved so well, and he still didn't know—couldn't possibly have known—that four years would pass before he was acquitted of those disgraceful charges.

Silvio Berlusconi, a mirror and a caricature of the Italians, the Stromboli of the last few days of summer holiday in Toyland—the happy, sedated country we thought we lived in and where, instead, *everything is broken up and dances*, as Jim Morrison warned us a million years ago.

Guido

AFTER GREECE, in the meantime, Ireland and Portugal too are forced to throw down their weapons in the face of the markets' onslaught, and they voluntarily surrender to the control of the troika—the European Commission, the European Central Bank, and the International Monetary Fund—which, in exchange for substantial loans (85 billion euros to Ireland and 78 billion to Portugal), demands that they approve the reforms required by the rules of austerity, namely a deadly cocktail of cuts to the social welfare safety nets and public spending and, at the same time, tax hikes on citizens and companies.

In the face of the slow but constant hemorrhaging of Spanish and Italian treasury bills, the European Central Bank—at the time headed by the Frenchman Jean-Claude Trichet—reacts with a surprising move: on April 8, 2011, the official interest rates of the euro are shifted a quarter point upward, rising from 1 percent to 1.25 percent, and on July 7, 2011, they rise even further, reaching 1.5 percent.

You ought to remember that date very clearly, Edoardo. That's the day you won the Strega Prize.

While America floods its markets with liquidity, Europe restricts credit, making it even more expensive. It's as if, aboard the *Titanic*, the captain had decided to solve the problem of the *atrocious heat* that the first-class passengers were complaining about by flooding steerage with ice-cold seawater.

Trichet's idea is to counterbalance certain invisible inflationistic forces that every German government fears like the plague, and has feared ever since the years of the Weimar Republic. But the interpretation that the markets put on it—for that matter, the only interpretation possible—is that the countries with a liquidity crisis are going to be abandoned to their fate.

This is the moment when the attack on Italy and Spain and the euro is well and truly unleashed. After Trichet's brilliant move, investors around the world start to buy German treasury bills and sell Italian and Spanish treasury bills—the same elementary and yet highly effective weapon that had already been turned against Greece. The spread between the treasury bills and the German Bunds experiences an immediate uptick, rising, in the month of July alone, from 180 basis points to more than 300, thus driving prohibitively high the interest rates on the bills Italy places on the markets every month in order to finance its current expenses. The same thing happens to Spain and its Bonos.

Ice-cold water starts to fill steerage, in other words, and during that sweltering hot summer I start to feel like a character in one of those apocalyptic American movies (I know it doesn't make me the most refined of film connoisseurs, but I've always loved them: *2012*, *The Day After Tomorrow*, *Deep Impact*, and even *Armageddon*), a character who knows about some impending catastrophe while the rest of mankind remains blissfully in the dark.

Of course, I can't and don't want to tell anyone. It wouldn't change anything, and after all, we know what a bad end Cassandra came to. My nights again become endless, though, and when I walk through Milan and Rome and watch people living the days of their lives normally, I ask myself what will happen when the situation worsens—because it's bound to get worse, the spread is bound to rise even further, and who can say how high it will go—and the truth comes out and everyone will be forced to come to terms with it.

What is the government going to do, what are the Italians, men and women, going to do? What are my family members, my employees going to do? What am I going to do?

One night my girlfriend confronts me, she asks me what's wrong. When I give her my usual evasive answer, she demands that I let her check my smartphone. Everything. My text messages, my email, my WhatsApp, my Facebook. She's convinced that I'm hiding who knows what kind of secret, maybe—who knows—a lover, and so I hand the phone over. She finds nothing, of course, and at that point I'm forced to tell her the truth. Explain to her the way I feel and why. How I'm forced to live behind a mask, while waiting for a disaster that will be impossible to avoid.

It does me good though, and for a while I feel better. Summer vacation comes, and most of Italy takes off work. It's no longer the whole month we were talking about above, but lots of people do get time off in 2011, too, maybe for just a week or so. Millions of people head off on summer vacation, tired but untroubled, worried only about the television newscasters reporting traffic jams on the stretch of superhighway they're planning to drive.

And then the dance begins.

Edoardo

I'D NEVER WON ANYTHING before in my life.

I remember the very short phone call in which Elisabetta Sgarbi informed me that we'd be competing for the prize, and that it would be nice if Sandro Veronesi and Antonio Pennacchi could present my book, but that I would have to call them immediately, and I was sitting in my parked car outside of the gymnasium where my son Ettore was learning to box, telling myself okay, okay, and blinking rapidly.

I remember the beauty and class and tremendous allure of Luciana Castellina, who was also competing for the prize, and the wonderful Irish linen blouse she wore, and how one evening, when she saw me arrive for dinner in a clearly non–Irish linen shirt that was far too rumpled, she whispered to me in no uncertain terms to go and find a new shirt immediately, and to put on a jacket while I was at it—a peremptory order that I obeyed immediately. Then she told me that Marshal Tito was a very handsome man.

I remember that my daughter Angelica took her ninth-grade final exams while I was away, and in that same period, Ettore went to London on his own for the first time, staying with his cousin Leonardo, who had rented an apartment in some sort of Jamaican ghetto, and he told me that on the street in front of his building there were framed photographs of young black men and boys with earrings who had been killed right there, and under the photos were vases with flowers, and the flowers were always fresh. When I ordered him to say nothing to his mother and to come home to Prato immediately, he laughed and told me there was no problem. He was having the time of his life, roaming the streets of that magnificent city all on his own.

"Dad, don't worry, everything's fine here. You just worry about winning."

I remember that the day before the final judging and announcement, while I was zipping along at 185 miles per hour on the bullet train, I read that Giorgio Manganelli said of Gabriele d'Annunzio—who had studied in Prato, at the same school I attended, the Cicognini National Boarding School—that "he belonged to the muddy and provincial or bullyish age of overbearing provincialism," and I wondered whether I too, deep down, wasn't just a provincial bully, an overbearing author who chooses to write about the things that matter to him and wants to win the Strega Prize anyway.

And then I remember the moment of the victory, while I was on the stage of the Ninfeo di Valle Giulia and Pennacchi proclaimed me the winner and Elisabetta looked over at me happily and deeply moved and the photographers called me by name and blinded me with their flashes, and I couldn't keep from thinking that if I'm standing on this stage it's entirely thanks to the story of the immense defeat that I suffered—the same as millions of people just like me, throughout Italy and throughout Europe—and when they asked me if I wanted to dedicate my Strega Prize to anyone, I answered that I dedicated it to Prato, my mar-ve-lous hometown.

That's exactly how I said it, like a lunatic, enunciating every syllable separately.

Guido

ON AUGUST 4, 2011, Jean-Claude Trichet and Mario Draghi (respectively, outgoing and incoming presidents of the European Central Bank) send a letter to Berlusconi. They recommend the immediate adoption of a series of reforms that would ensure Italy the support of the ECB. These reforms need to be implemented immediately, by a decree law, and Parliament must approve them by September.

The Berlusconi administration stammered. It stalled for time. For that matter, it was being asked to do the impossible: his majority wouldn't go along with him. The summer went by fast, too fast, and for all of September and October the spread remained constant between 300 and 400 points. The big thing people were waiting for was the outcome of the G-20 summit meeting in Cannes, in preparation for which the Italian prime minister responded to Draghi and Trichet's letter with another letter, in which he committed to start adopting some of the recommended reforms.

In the stock photographs from the summit, Berlusconi appears to be beaming but all alone, ignored by his fellow leaders and kept at bay by his own minister of the economy. He knew that his days as prime minister were coming to an end and he courageously refused the offer of aid from the International Monetary Fund, but he couldn't turn down an outside supervision of the implementation of the reforms just adopted, concerning which—both José Manuel Barroso (for the European Commission) and Christine Lagarde (for the International Monetary Fund) explained—there was *an issue of credibility*.

At the final press conference for the summit, he says:

> We believe that it really will prove to be a short-lived fad, this tendency of the markets to go after Italy's sovereign debt securities. We truly are a powerful economy, the third-biggest European economy, the world's seventh-biggest. Life in Italy is life in a prosperous country. This is shown to be true all the time. Consumer spending hasn't declined, the restaurants are full…Air travel…it's hard to get reservations for flights…Vacation spots on long weekends are absolutely overbooked. Well, I just can't imagine that if you come to live in Italy you'd

get any impression that Italy is suffering through anything that might resemble a real downturn...

When asked to explain further, he admits that, certainly, there has been "some impoverishment of a significant sector of the Italian population," but the blame should be put entirely on the exchange rate between the Italian lira and the euro which was set by the Prodi government, nine years earlier.

Before he's even done speaking, the markets lunge at Italy. This time it's all the investors in the world, and they hit hard. Just five days later, on November 9, 2011, the spread hits a historic high of 575, taking the yield on the ten-year treasury bill to 7.47 percent and, basically, shutting off Italy's access to the credit markets.

It's an unsustainable situation; the disaster that I've feared for so long has finally arrived. Outside of Italy, there is no longer anyone willing to buy our treasury bills, and the Italian state can no longer refinance itself: soon there won't even be the resources to pay retirement pensions and the salaries of government employees.

These are dramatic times. The size of our debt and our economy threatens the very survival of the euro and the European Union. Perhaps we're on the brink of a collapse of the world financial system, because if it was a political impossibility but still quantitatively possible to rescue Greece, rescuing Italy is simply impossible.

Three days later Silvio Berlusconi, the prime minister, tenders his resignation to the president of the Italian

Republic, Giorgio Napolitano, and I'm sitting in front of the TV, like millions of Italians, watching video of a jubilant crowd celebrating in front of the Quirinal Palace, residence of the president.

I now don't know what to think. That spontaneous display of emotion surprises me greatly. There's a delight and a joy on display that strikes fear in my heart. They're celebrating the defeat of a man who has always seemed like a tyrant to them, certainly, and maybe they now think that all their problems have been solved. But that, unfortunately, is not the case. They have no idea what awaits them. For that matter, no one does.

Instead of Berlusconi, Mario Monti arrives, and when the illustrious professor from Bocconi University and former European commissioner appears before the Chamber of Deputies to take up his duties as Italy's new prime minister, he is greeted with a burst of cheers and applause louder and more enthusiastic than any heard previously in that chamber.

The professor turns down the assistance offered by the troika and instead wholeheartedly embraces the austerity program, forcing a very harsh economic recovery plan consisting of a mix of taxes and budget cuts through a terrified Italian Parliament. The plan is called "Save Italy" and it wins the support of the markets and the European Commission, and assistance from the European Central Bank.

A few weeks later, in fact, as soon as Draghi is seated officially as governor, he starts the LTRO (Long Term

Refinancing Operation): a low-interest offer of cash made by the ECB to every bank in Europe that believes it is in need of that cash. There is no limit set on the amount: the banks will be able to borrow all the cash they feel they require, to be reimbursed in three years. As collateral for these loans, the ECB demands treasury bills of the various European states.

It's not the same as the quantitative easing introduced three years earlier by the Federal Reserve, because they're not printing money. It's just a gigantic refinancing operation, with set expiration dates. In fact, banks are being given money so they can buy European treasury bills. It seems like a perfect mechanism, because at one fell swoop they are refinancing the banks, propping up the market in government securities, assuring the success of the new security issues, and frightening away speculators.

In a few months' time, the ECB lends out a trillion euros and, in the face of such overwhelming firepower, the speculative attack is abandoned and the last few profits are pocketed while the spreads drop sharply.

In Italy, in the meantime, Monti's austerity strikes hard: the cuts that he imposes on the country are Carverian, and they not only slice into living flesh, they don't even stop at the bone: they go all the way down to the marrow. Italian society at large and the country's morale are both hit very hard by the simultaneous impact of the reintroduction of the home tax that Berlusconi had removed, the reform—that is, the tightening—of pensions, and the increase in the value-added tax (VAT).

Suddenly, everything screeches to a halt. Consumer spending halts, prices halt, investment decisions halt. The real estate market comes to a halt too, and so does the market for cars. Shops of every kind and level of quality start gasping for air. Even spending on groceries drops.

The battle that Monti starts to fight, with no quarter given, against tax evasion, in which our country leads the world, is waged with a strength and determination that no Italian leader had ever deployed before, but it winds up terribly worsening the difficulties that the country faces.

Troubled by the looming threat of an Italian default to which they hear ominous references every other day from the new prime minister, catapulted unexpectedly into a grim new reality of shortages and hardship, the Italians withdraw to their homes and put off all purchases that aren't absolutely necessary. Terrified by the possibility of being stopped on the street by the Italian tax authorities and forced to prove, tax returns in hand, that their reported income was sufficient to justify the purchase of the car they are driving, the Italians give in to a pessimism that has always been alien to their nature and their history.

Every desire becomes a guilty sin, every outlay can be postponed, every whim a frivolous waste, all wealth suspect, and anyway, best to keep things undercover and hidden, in part out of the fear you might run into one of those blanket audits by the financial police that looks like nothing so much as an all-out raid, and seems to be visited with a special vengeance upon every business establishment with so much as a whiff of tax evasion about it: from the most unassuming neighborhood cafés to high-end boutiques on Via Montenapoleone, from discotheques to restaurants, butcher's shops to grocery stores to flower stands to beauty parlors to woodworking shops, everyone and everything is under scrutiny, even the ships out at sea, and massive, ruinous fines are levied against proprietors and customers unable to show official receipts, their names fed to the newspapers so they can be offered up as examples.

They want to teach honesty and sobriety to the country beloved around the world as the best place to live. And the country learns its lesson. It learns its lesson all too well. It doesn't spend another euro.

A few months later, the Spanish prime minister Mariano Rajoy announces that Spain will not be able to respect the 3 percent limit on the deficit-to-GDP ratio, but instead will hit 5.8 percent. The Spanish banks are once again subjected to pressure, weighed down as they are by the aftermath of the real estate crunch, and Madrid's treasury bills are once again at the eye of the storm, taking with them their Italian counterparts.

In the second half of July, the two countries' spreads once again spike above—well above—500 points, and once again the euro seems to be on the verge of crashing.

On July 26, 2012, in London, Mario Draghi takes the floor at the Global Investment Conference: a not particularly important appointment on the calendar of the financial world, but which, this year, will go down in history.

Edoardo

STREET FIGHTS OBEY CERTAIN IRONCLAD RULES, and I had a friend who was an expert. In those moments of absolute uncertainty when each potential combatant is weighing the courage and intentions of the potential adversaries and it still remains unclear whether there is even going to be a brawl, he would always address his adversary with the same, very brief phrase: "I'm going to hit you."

The mere simple announcement that my friend was ready to start throwing punches often persuaded the young men he was facing off with that it might be better to try to talk it out. Suddenly it erased the thought that they might be able to get out of that quarrel unharmed, forcing them to reflect on the likelihood they would be taking at least one punch to the face.

He was just explaining the risk, is all my friend was doing. In fact, he was presenting that risk in the flesh. And when he said, "I'm going to hit you," it always worked. It inevitably put an end to things. Every time.

When Mario Draghi starts speaking, he's only filmed by the TV cameras present at the conference. It's a real pity that this wasn't live TV, but then, it never is when the really important things happen.

His voice is steady, but he seems tired. There's a hint of dark circles under his eyes, and even his hair, usually so carefully combed that it seems sculpted, looks a little messy: two little shocks of hair stick out of the carefully brushed mass, defiant cowlicks—as defiant as Mario Draghi's hair can ever be, let's be clear about it, we're not talking about Axl Rose here. And on closer inspection, even the part isn't perfect. He seems to have parted his hair himself, in front of the mirror, a couple of hours earlier.

He starts off by saying that the euro and the eurozone are both much stronger than is generally recognized, and that in the past six months they have made extraordinary progress, both at the national and the supranational level.

He explains that all the countries of Europe, including the United Kingdom, have asked to have more Europe, not less Europe, and they've accepted shared fiscal regulations.

He adds that he often hears people talk about the euro's fragility, and even a euro crisis, and he emphasizes that certain political leaders of countries that don't belong to the eurozone frequently underestimate the sheer quantity of political capital that has been invested in the euro, and the fact that the euro is irreversible.

And then he says that he has a message to convey: "Within our mandate, the ECB is ready to do whatever it takes to preserve the euro." He takes a brief pause, then he resumes. "And believe me, it will be enough."

From the footage, you can see that the man is aware that he's talking big. It's very clear that he's not entirely certain he's going to be able to keep the immense promise he's just made. His voice is calm, but his figure doesn't radiate that aura of authority we're accustomed to today. For that matter, this is still a moment *before*, this is the moment when Draghi *becomes* Draghi. The moment that will turn him into a giant in a world of midgets.

He goes on, calmly explaining that the spreads are interfering with the proper functioning of the channels of transmission of monetary policy, and therefore with the ECB's mandate. And that the ECB will be forced to deal with them, too.

"I think I will stop here," he concludes, "I think my assessment was candid and frank enough."

"I'm going to hit you," Mario Draghi says to everyone, and to each of the investors around the world. And the crisis of the euro ends there, at that moment.

II. THE ICE AGE

Edoardo

ON FEBRUARY 24 AND 25, 2013, Italy holds political elections, and I'm elected to the Chamber of Deputies.

The story of how I wound up in the Italian Parliament is short and convulsive. It involves my love for Italy, my books, the Strega Prize and the brand-new burst of popularity that accrued to me as a result of that prize, Luca di Montezemolo, Mario Monti, and above all the scorching realization that *something could and had to be done, and that the time to act had come.*

It all began on November 17, 2012, in Rome, when I accepted an invitation to a sort of political event with the ambitious and, at the same time, stale and tired title of Toward the Third Republic, which in the intentions of its organizers was supposed to serve as a launching board for a new centrist party, composed only and exclusively of people from the so-called *civil society*, and to be led by Montezemolo, then Ferrari's CEO.

Seven thousand people came from all over Italy, and I was the first speaker. I looked out at that huge crowd, and I compared it to the few dozen intrepid aficionados who, when things are going well, show up for book readings. I took a deep breath and warmed up, ready to spout what strike me today as fervent, candid, naive statements that, then and there, struck me as neither fervent nor candid nor naive, not in the slightest.

How do you give shape to a proper, necessary, obligatory protest without having to resort to extreme forms — without resorting to violence, either physical or conceptual? Is it possible to be angry, indignant, furious, without reducing oneself to calling for revolutions, real or imaginary? Is it possible to maintain the necessary sangfroid to reform the system in depth without going so far as to destroy it? Can one dismiss with contempt those who were wrong or incompetent or untrustworthy or even genuine crooks, without at the same time also chasing away those — and there were a great many of them, even in the machinery of state — who did good work? Where does the new broom stop sweeping clean? Because there can be no doubt that there's need of a new broom. You can't think that those who broke the toy are capable of fixing it. That's not the way it works. Then who is going to do it? Maybe we have to do it ourselves.

We who come from a civil society and wonder whether it's possible, opportune, and right to commit to the reform of politics. We who aren't politicians and have never wanted to be. We who have always thought that we could be useful to our families and to our country by simply doing our work. We who know very well how infinitely easier it is to protest than it is to change things, to break rather than build. We who are here today and who, whether we like it or not, feel the weight of representing millions of people who are lost, who have no political representation and who therefore feel themselves to be courted and blandished on all sides. We who still have some hope.

It was true. I had the hope and the conviction that the decline of Italy's economy and society might not prove irreversible, and the certainty that in order to fight that decline it was absolutely necessary to become involved in politics. I thought that I could represent the voice and the anger of people like me, who had lost everything, in a venue where no one runs the risk of losing anything, save perhaps their honor.

The event was successful, and starting on that day, everything seemed to pick up speed. When the elections were imminent, Luca di Montezemolo decided not to announce his candidacy and handed over his movement to that same Mario Monti whom I had criticized so harshly in my books. And yet, when we finally met,

Mario Monti first made it clear that he had read those books, and then gave me a life lesson I have not since forgotten, asking me what else he could have done as Italy's leader, in the dramatic and harrowing situation in which he'd found himself governing the country.

I'm convinced that at some point in the future the acrimony that so many Italians claim to feel toward Professor Monti's political actions will become more tempered; I feel sure that they will recognize that Professor Monti did meritorious service to his country by yanking back from the precipice—albeit with harsh measures—an economy that was on the verge of plummeting into the void.

Back then, though, I told myself that I couldn't dream of running for office on the electoral list of the leading supporter of austerity policies. Not me. Not with what I'd lived through. Not with the way I thought about things. Not with the things I'd written. And then, if there was a politician I liked, it was Matteo Renzi—the young mayor of Florence who had invited me to speak at the Stazione Leopolda and had just lost the Democratic Party (PD) primaries.

I couldn't sleep and I couldn't relax. I didn't have much time to make up my mind whether to run, and not everyone in my family agreed. On the other hand, the polls said that you could stick a fork in Berlusconi, because he was done, that Beppe Grillo would get 10 percent of the vote at the very most, and that the alliance between this electoral list of the civil society, still nameless, and the PD would win hands down and put Italy back on track after the disastrous years of Berlusconi's government.

Maybe, I said to myself, there really was a chance of doing something useful besides writing. Perhaps, if I ran for office, I could find a way to make sure that my desperate defense of small businesses and those who still worked for them could find the ear of *colà dove si puote*, a reference from Dante to the highest power of the Almighty. Because there necessarily had to be a second phase in Monti's political process, I thought: after ensuring the country's safety, it would certainly be necessary to ensure there was a recovery, and if I was being asked to run for office—I kidded myself—then perhaps my desperate defense had already found an audience, and perhaps it could even become one of the few, intensely necessary hinges in a government effort that truly worked to get the country back on its feet.

It would be necessary to get my hands dirty, no doubt about it. To set off on an adventure that might last as long as five years and would keep me far from my home and my family. I'd have to go live in Rome and work at Palazzo Montecitorio, the seat of the Italian Chamber of Deputies. I'd have to go write laws instead of novels, a job I had no training for and which I wasn't sure I knew how to do. I'd have to join a party and represent it in the Parliament, I who have never joined anything, and find myself working alongside people I didn't know but whose words and actions I might still have to answer for in the future. It was a leap into the void, exactly the kind of thing I'd never attempted or wanted to attempt in my life.

After one last sleepless night, I accepted and immediately found myself catapulted into a brief, empty, and vicious election campaign, although it was at least somewhat simplified by an election law that made it virtually certain that I and anyone else who like me was the first on a list of candidates would be elected.

Many of the people I met—all the entrepreneurs, all the businessmen, with no exceptions—disagreed that Monti had saved Italy, they thought he'd ruined it, and it was impossible to get them to change their minds. National polling seemed to reflect these opinions: every day our numbers looked worse and worse. What's more, Monti wasn't especially effective on television—unlike Berlusconi, who didn't seem to have any detectable fork sticking in him or to be done at all—while on the other hand it was by now certain that Grillo, what with all his shouting, was bound to take much more than 10 percent.

When voting day finally rolled around, I wasn't even in Italy. Many months earlier, I had agreed to go and do a book presentation for *Story of My People*, the English edition of my book which had won the Strega Prize, *in Kansas City*. I know, it seems like a joke, but while Italy was voting I had an obligation to keep, and I found myself as the guest of a major book fair in Missouri—because, inexplicably to an Italian, half of Kansas City is in Kansas and half is in Missouri—sitting on a podium talking about the disasters of globalization with booksellers from San

Francisco and Dallas, while on the podium next to mine Dave Eggers was presenting *Your Fathers, Where Are They? And the Prophets, Do They Live Forever?* and I risked being snowed in by the imminent arrival of a massive blizzard that I just barely managed to outrun, only to hear a feverish account from my friend Federico Guarducci, as I was boarding a plane for Italy in Atlanta, about how the early projections were announcing unbelievable results, with the Five Star Movement and Forza Italia battling equally with the Democratic Party to win the majority dividend that belonged to the party that came in first, while Scelta Civica, or Civil Choice—that was the miserable name that had been given to our electoral list—was taking well under 10 percent.

Upon landing in Rome after a flight that seemed never to end, when I powered up my cell phone I found it flooded with dozens of text messages and voice mails congratulating me. Italy was ungovernable, and I had been elected.

Guido

IN THE MEANTIME, the celestial machinery Malcolm
Lowry wrote about had continued to spin for years, click-
ing along undisturbed, and it had engendered events and
coincidences that turned the world into a completely different place from the one we'd lived in way back in 2000,
so much so that the central banks of the United Kingdom, Japan, and, in the end, even the European Central
Bank found themselves forced to follow the example of
the Federal Reserve, and had started to print money.

Ten trillion dollars were created over the course of
a few years by global quantitative easing, money that
was to be pumped into the financial system. That's such

a huge number that it's hard to imagine or calculate—more or less four times Italy's national debt. In the hopes of the governors of the central banks, the sheer immensity of this mass of new money was meant to bury under its weight all existing financial crises, as well as ward off future ones.

The plan works, and it succeeds in stabilizing the system: interest rates drop, stock markets start to rise more or less everywhere, and the spreads between the various European countries come back under control, restoring the euro to safety. It seems like the ideal remedy for the catastrophe that had been looming, the perfect weapon against all speculation: in fact, no one can dream of going up against this kind of firepower, especially because it's endlessly renewable.

Quantitative easing (QE), however, can't go on indefinitely: when in October 2014 the Federal Reserve—which of course had been the first to start, after the collapse of Lehman Brothers—decides to stop printing dollars, the United States finds itself with a banking system that has been restored to stability and an economy that has once again started to chug.

In America, in fact, QE also seemed to work for companies and people, not just for banks. In a society based on the universal reliance on debt, even the slightest drop in the interest rate automatically affects every loan, every mortgage, every lease and instalment plan, bringing relief and renewed energy to consumers and manufacturers, who can rely upon the services of a much more efficient and stratified financial market than we have in Europe, which relies chiefly upon bank loans.

In the United States, moreover, the difficult transition between the old economy and the new economy has by and large been completed already: many of those who've lost their jobs in manufacturing have already found another in the lower ranks of digital companies, without swelling the ranks of the army of the jobless that is such a blight upon the face of Europe. As far as official statistics are concerned, it little matters that all these people are now overqualified, that from the specialized workers they used to be, they now find themselves working as drivers—mere interchangeable cogs in the great new basin of logistics created by the mechanism of online markets—and having to settle for the measly wages paid to the van drivers that deliver to your door everything that's purchased on the Internet—because all you need to drive a van is a driver's license, not a college degree.

In Europe, on the other hand, no one has the nerve to test Draghi's resolve and so, beginning on that day in late July 2012 and for the three years that follow, the European Central Bank does very little. Practically speaking, the ECB sits down to wait for the repayment of the trillion euros it has loaned out to banks with the LTRO.

The problem of a real economy at its last gasp nearly everywhere across Europe isn't dealt with at all, but since simply ignoring a problem that afflicts millions of people isn't enough to solve it, in June 2014 the ECB makes up its mind to launch the TLTROs (Targeted Longer-Term

Refinancing Operations), a financing plan that offers particularly advantageous rates to banks that agree to finance individuals and small businesses.

On paper, it looks like a good idea, but in practice it obtains few if any results: the banks are reluctant to lend to industrial sectors (in other words, manufacturing) and companies (small businesses) that have already filled those banks' balance sheets with collection problems, and even though there are few businessmen even willing to invest in this economic climate, those few find themselves facing a brick wall.

In order to get those loans, of course, it is necessary to have credentials as a "virtuous" debtor. In other words, you need to have clear and demonstrable financial solidity that attests to your ability to honor the obligations assumed with the debt. But the very same underpinnings of austerity—the tightening of consumption, the downward pressure on wages, precarization of labor—associated with the barbaric competition deriving from globalization, mean that these people and companies aren't capable of providing the banks with sufficient guarantees, and they therefore refuse to extend credit to small businesses, thereby rendering useless and ineffective the lowering of interest rates.

In other words, the horse won't drink, and it isn't until March 2015, immediately following the end of the LTRO, that the ECB, having just received repayment of the trillion euros it lent to the banks in 2012, decides to launch its own quantitative easing.

The APP, or asset purchase program, is the name of the European quantitative easing, and it's an ambitious plan for the direct, open-market purchase of treasury bills issued by eurozone nations; it can also be expanded to take in securities issued by private companies, bonds and even stocks.

The first expansive monetary maneuver in European history, though, consists of throwing a life preserver to the countries in trouble, while the companies and the citizens of most of those countries are left to fend for themselves in the stormy seas of the economic downturn, and practically kept in the dark about the very existence of such an immense financial maneuver.

Yes, because out of all the billions of euros that are printed by the ECB, almost none of that money trickles down to the real economy: conjured out of nothing, it remains hovering in midair like a cloud of some sort, invisible and imprisoned, and remains there to finance the immense debt of the individual countries and to prop up the debts of their banks, tried and tested by years of financial crisis and poor management and titanic mountains of bad debt.

This was not an arrogant decision made by the cruel, sharp-clawed masters of the world's banks, motivated by their hatred of ordinary people. It was a necessity. The banks—all the banks in Europe—had to be rescued, whatever the cost, because it was in their coffers that the savings of Europe's citizens were safeguarded, as well as billions in state treasury bills, and no one was interested in seeing runs on banks in all the capitals of the Old World.

And anyway, there was no way around it. The mandate of the ECB is prevalently bound up with inflation, and the monetary interventions required to reduce the spread between creditor nations and debtor nations make use of, and already in a certain sense dictate, the boundaries of the domain in which the ECB is able to intervene.

This is what it can do, this is what it must do. Nothing more.

And in fact the very powerful nations of Northern Europe don't like QE one bit. They are successful in delaying its implementation to some extent, but in the end they're forced to grin and bear it. How many times did we hear them say that by adopting QE, Mario Draghi is pushing, if not actually exceeding, the boundaries of his powers?

Brandishing their textbooks, they continuously warn against the danger of kindling the dread inflation that always comes with every influx of new money into the system, though they console themselves with the thought that, along with the help that QE brings to the balance sheets of the most heavily indebted countries, there will also come the sacrifices of austerity and their immediate consequences for the citizens of those countries: cuts in the public sector, a tightening of pensions, taxes on consumers goods, the precarization of labor.

They're convinced that it is only through these sacrifices that the grasshopper states—so they have now been dubbed, in the umpteenth trite animalistic metaphor— will be able to get their debt under control and improve their balance sheets. It's the only reason the Northern

Europeans are willing to tolerate the continuance of that onanistic mechanism by means of which the ECB prints euros to buy treasury bills.

To them it would be inconceivable and entirely unacceptable—even laughable—to consider putting in place a financing plan to transfer money directly from the central bank to small businesses and individual people. Our German friends would immediately ask us: There must be a reason that the small businesses in the Mediterranean region are undergoing a liquidity crisis, right? We do live in a global world, or have you forgotten? If the money can't be handed over by the banks in their own territory, why should we have the ECB entrust it to them? And what collateral could these companies hope to offer to the Eurotower in Frankfurt? Looms, vans, circular saws, sample books? To say nothing of people, after all…

And so, to borrow the words of David Foster Wallace, the snowfall of QE money falls on the map of the world, rather than on the real world. On the immaterial institutions that command the world, instead of on the citizens who actually live in it.

The great blizzard of money, in fact, piles up atop the small and midsized companies of non-German Europe without ever actually touching them, and then it hardens and becomes a dome—an igloo that hibernates what remains of the European middle class, deleting all and any hopes of social mobility.

The future dies, and the Ice Age begins.

Edoardo

THEY'D TOLD ME, of course.

I had been told plenty of times that on the first day of the new parliament, I wasn't going to be carried on the shoulders of my cheering new colleagues, and conducted triumphantly to Palazzo Chigi and acclaimed prime minister, but what I certainly couldn't have expected was that once I became a member of Parliament I would do practically nothing for the next two months, the time that it took Pierluigi Bersani to surrender to the necessity of a grand-coalition government, under the leadership of Enrico Letta. It was fiercely opposed from the very first minute of the very first day by the unflagging obstructionism and the extemporaneous protests of the parliamentarians of the populist Five Star Movement, who used every opportunity to turn a speech on the floors into accusations of robbery and theft against their fellow members of Parliament, whatever their party, and once even trooped down en masse to take over the government benches, invading them for a spectacular photo opportunity, which they then followed up a few days later by sending an intrepid phalanx of Five Star MPs to occupy the roofs of Palazzo Montecitorio, accompanied by shouts of "Honesty! Honesty!"

In those two months, it became evident that the reason I ran for office in the first place—*that burning idea that something could and had to be done, and that this was the right moment to do it*—was just a good applause line designed to be used at meetings of Confindustria, the national employers' federation and chamber of commerce. Entering politics in order to bring change is a slogan that—centuries old though it may be—can still get you into the Chamber of Deputies, but actually bringing change into a system as closed as the one that encloses the countries of Europe is a titanic undertaking and, from what I saw, an impossible one.

It's certainly not from Palazzo Montecitorio that anything can be done to stop the movement of the celestial machinery, and the phases of disenchantment are more or less these: first you realize that an individual member of Parliament can do nothing, then that your party can do nothing, then that no party—not even the majority party—can do anything, then that the government can do nothing, and at last you realize that Italian politics as a whole can do nothing.

In a few months Civil Choice suffered a schism and then disbanded, leaving politically homeless that ambitious, failed contingent of prominent names from industry and business, the major professions and the leading universities, which had sallied forth in all its pomp and circumstance to the political elections *in order to fight against the decline of the Italian economy and society.*

When a discouraged Mario Monti tendered his resignation from the very party he had founded to join the Senate's mixed group, I called him. I told him that I understood, and that I would be doing the same thing.

I wasn't going to stay in the mixed group long either, I thought. Just enough time to let the froth of my disappointment subside and clarify my thoughts, then I'd resign from Parliament entirely. I hadn't just chosen the wrong party, I'd made a mistake by running for office in the first place. There was nothing left but to present a round of apologies and go back home, passing through the humiliating gauntlet of the lengthy and complicated procedure required for a member of Parliament to resign, which instead of being the relatively painless consequence of that MP's decision, constitutes some sort of a full-fledged public act of contrition.

I tried to write my letter of resignation to Speaker Laura Boldrini. I must have written a dozen drafts, and I crumpled them all up.

The harder I tried to explain why I wanted to quit, the weaker my motives seemed in contrast with the sheer scope of the fact that—ridiculous though the election law might be, rigged though the lists of candidates might be, though the party might have disintegrated, powerless though politics might be to actually do anything—I had still been elected *to represent the people*, and I couldn't just duck out of such an elevated and ancient and noble and romantic commitment, simply because it had occurred to me that I had never wanted to be or become a politician.

I'd accepted a responsibility and I had to maintain that commitment and see it through, no matter what happened and however useless I might feel. I certainly wasn't going to be able to halt the celestial machinery Malcolm Lowry wrote about, but the Parliament isn't there only to work on the economy, and I wanted and was duty-bound to contribute to passing certain necessary laws, like the one on civil union, Italy's equivalent of gay marriage, the Dopo Di Noi legislation concerning the treatment of disabled children after the death of their parents, and the law on end-of-life ethics.

To avoid misgivings and controversy I decided that I wouldn't join another party, and I resolved to serve out the legislative term where I now sat, in the mixed group, that exquisitely neutral refuge that includes those who have found themselves so at odds with the party they originally ran with that they are forced to leave it, condemning themselves to the vise grip of digital ostracism and political shunning over the course of the legislative session, almost always undermining their future careers.

Among the renegades, easy targets for the cruder sorts of commentators and lashed relentlessly by a public opinion that was hungry for scapegoats, I felt right at home.

We are a handful of freaks (politically speaking, of course), made up of standard-bearers for linguistic minorities, advocates of independence for Sardinia or the Po Valley or the Venetian region, former Communists, former Fascists, individualists, turncoats, idealists, sly dogs, heirs to the tradition of major parties swept away by history, native Italians elected with votes from Italians living overseas, sole representatives of old parties long since dead and buried—people who are frequently free and proud, often disappointed and almost always defeated, who have nothing in common with each other save that they've washed up and found a haven in this improbable, highly variegated community of misfits that, on certain days, reminds me of the assembly of oddballs in the cantina scene in *Star Wars*, while on others it evokes the brotherhood of losers who are hiding out in the sweet, lost Vineland in Thomas Pynchon's book of that name—a book that, by the way, you should read right away, *Vineland*.

In their midst, and like them, I perform my duties as a member of Parliament, and on certain days I still manage to feel pride in what I'm doing. I've stopped wondering how much my vote can count in the midst of the other 629 members, male and female, of one of the world's largest lower houses; I've stopped wondering just how legitimate my term in office can really be now that the constitutional court has overturned as illegitimate the election law under which I was voted into Parliament, or whether this commitment of three days a week at an absurdly high rate of pay can fairly be considered work, and during the endless waits in the Transatlantico—the long corridor with stunningly high ceilings and a floor in travertine limestone embellished with yellow Sienna marble inlays which extends in both directions, pointlessly majestic, outside the legislative chamber—to which we are condemned by the archaic regulations of the Chamber of Deputies, I no longer ask myself, as Bruce Chatwin once did, what I'm doing here.

I know what I'm doing here. I'm voting.

I vote for the laws that are introduced in the chamber, of course, because in my condition as a wildcat parliamentarian, an MP without a party, I'd rather not introduce any bills of my own, because they'd be moot in any case, guaranteed never to progress to the floor of the chamber for debate.

I vote more than fourteen thousand times. I vote for amendments and items on the agenda. I vote for motions and resolutions. I vote to ratify international treaties. I vote to approve reports from commissions of inquiry, including the one on the newly established commission on the kidnapping and death of Aldo Moro.

I vote in favor of the Letta government, the Renzi government, and the Gentiloni government. I vote to elect the members of the Consiglio superiore della magistratura (CSM, or High Council of the Judiciary). I vote to elect the judges of the constitutional court. I vote to elect the speaker of the Chamber of Deputies. I vote to elect the president of the Italian Republic, twice. First for Giorgio Napolitano and then for Sergio Mattarella.

I vote. That's what I agreed to do, and that's what I do. I vote.

Guido

AND WHILE EDOARDO IS BUSY VOTING, quantitative easing runs like a steamroller over every economic theory
and establishes itself as the new law of the empire, because,
however impossible it may be to imagine it reigning in
perpetuity, it is equally difficult to imagine an easy way out
of the sole mechanism capable of frustrating and defying
the speculative attacks on such unsustainable national debts
as Italy's.

In a European system so heavily indebted and incapable of producing any significant economic growth,
there exists no other way of ensuring the solvency of certain key countries so as to guarantee the survival of the

European Union itself, and the stability of their political viability.

Basically, the governments of the most heavily indebted nations have no options. They are forced to accept the extortionate conditions, thereby putting at risk the future of the next generation in order to save the present of this generation, underwriting QE by approving the austerity measures that cannot be separated from it, at the cost of putting the real economy into a deep freeze. It little matters that the European Central Bank thus becomes a laboratory for monetary experimentation, or that this system is guided by a set of utterly absurd assumptions.

That's right, because even though it was decided upon and independently launched by the central bank, QE still has to comply with the rules of European Union policies. That means that it's not the underpinning support for struggling nations that one might assume it's only logical to implement: in fact, the purchases of treasury bills are carried out for every state in the eurozone, and they are made proportionately to the shares of capital that each of those nations holds in the ECB.

Which means that most of the purchases made by the central bank focus on *German* treasury bills, which certainly have no need of being propped up, since for years they've been enormously sought after and purchased as a shelter investment for money managers around the world.

The massive buying campaign soon raises the price of all those securities, and necessarily lowers their yield, but in the case of the German Bund, so high a price is soon reached that the yield drops to nothing. Zilch. A yield of zero.

Once the initial excitement dies down over this entirely new possibility of issuing euro bonds with a yield of zero, and after the celebrations of the umpteenth, inevitable spike in the stock markets, articles start to proliferate in the world's leading financial publications expressing a worrisome doubt: How can we live in a world where bond yields are zero? How will banks and insurance companies and pension funds and generally speaking all those businesses that are required to guarantee an active return to their investors even be able to survive? If there are no returns from the bond market, where is this money going to be invested? Will it all go into the stock market? And if not there, where?

No one knows the answer. Logically enough, since nothing of the sort has ever happened before. The truly revolutionary nature of QE can be found in the fact that there are no precedents or studies or theories that we can turn to. We're in uncharted territory, once again, and the market can only stand by in astonishment while the yield on all European treasury bills slowly sinks toward zero, and though this may be immensely helpful for the balance sheets of the most heavily indebted nations, because it allows them to issue new debt at rates that have never been so low, German securities and those of other virtuous nations actually cheerfully plunge downward through the positive yield barrier, ultimately offering (to use the term advisedly) a negative yield to their purchasers.

This means that an investor no longer receives a coupon on his German Bunds, but instead every year loses a certain sum for the privilege of keeping German-issued state securities in his portfolio.

Naturally, the drop in rates on treasury bills affects active bank rates, too, and as a result, in every European nation—not only in Germany or in the other nations of Northern Europe—the yield on checking accounts drops to zero, and, if you consider the various charges that accrue, keeping your money in a bank winds up *costing money*.

Therefore, paradoxically, investing in treasury bills is a losing venture. Maintaining liquidity becomes a losing venture. The only way of avoiding the depreciation of your money is to convert it to cash and keep it in a safe deposit box, the way merchants did in the Renaissance.

It would be appropriate here to note that, unlike Americans, Europeans—and especially Italians—are a population that tends to save. Of them, a great many are elderly and retired—the very core of the middle class, people who retired from the working world with a nest egg, the returns from which help them eke out their pension, allowing them and their families to live at least comfortably.

When interest rates were sufficiently high, few or none of these people would invest in businesses that entailed risk—whether that was a café or a shop, a real estate agency or a micro-company—because they'd earn much more from the low but reliable yield on treasury bills: a very widespread investment, which also enjoyed substantial tax benefits.

In Italy, where the treasury bills were called BOT, or *buoni del tesoro*, people referred to these investors as BOT people, with an obvious joking reference to the "boat people" who fled Vietnam after the end of the war there. They were the crucial counterpart of a social compromise that was perhaps ill-advised because it disincentivized private initiative, but still ensured the refinancing of the public debt.

There were millions of them, and they enjoyed a more than acceptable quality of life. Having worked all their lives, and being able to rely on a pension system that had been conceived so as to reward them, they were able to pay for their children to attend university, and to support them until they took their degree.

They had been the backbone of the Italian economy and the European economy, its piggy bank and living proof that the system worked and could create the most widely shared wealth possible. It fed much of the country's domestic demand and constituted one of the reasons — perhaps the principal reason — that Italy never witnessed the proliferation of those trailer parks which are so common in the heart of the American manufacturing belt that's been hit so hard by globalization. In the last harsh years of the economic downturn, moreover, their savings had also been used to help out those in their families, whether children or grandchildren, who'd been unable to find jobs.

All at once, with the arrival of negative interest rates, these people's every financial certainty is shattered: their purchasing power is annihilated, while their basic living expenses (electricity, gas, water) continue to climb, turning into genuine hidden taxes that eventually snuff out domestic demand entirely.

So that's how the European QE works. It saves the states, it helps the banks, and it ignores the real economy. It rises above politics and transcends it, becoming a sort of global constitution that has never been voted on by anyone, but it organizes and directs the governance of countries that rely upon it for their survival, forcing them into a relationship of absolute dependency.

Don't think I'm exaggerating here! How else could we describe a power or an authority capable of constraining a nation's executives to govern and legislate only and exclusively in directions permitted by that power or authority's dictates? We can only call it a *constituent* power or authority, such as is normally derived from a constitution.

The power of the QE, then, could be described as biopolitical for all the power it has to affect the lives of millions of people and for the way it manages to bypass politics completely, making it less and less important and influential and increasingly overestimated in Italy and in Europe.

Starving for justice, the army of invisibles prepares to invade the parliaments, but what can the parliaments do, what can democracy do against a limitless, immaterial

power, never elected and therefore impossible to over-
throw, and which however hated and illogical and regres-
sive and deflationary it may be, and even though it's a
bottomless source of ever greater inequality among the
populace, also remains the sole, perhaps the last bastion of
salvation against chaos?

Edoardo

MAYBE THE TIME HAS COME to admit that we've lost our desperate, sentimental, Luddite war against the world and against the future. To admit that we're going to have to settle for living in a country where a new, bloodless version of that neutron bomb has exploded, the N-bomb that we feared so much in the years of the Cold War—a piece of silent, cruel ordnance that left us alive and with our memories intact while it slaughtered all and every material ambition we'd ever had, our every all-too-human dream of prosperity.

Ah, it would take good old Ionesco to tell the tale of this world gone insane as it creaks and groans! In the same period of time that the ECB is printing 60 billion euros a month and using the cash to buy treasury bills, finding financing is virtually impossible for both small businesses and private citizens: lines of credit are turned down, mortgages are unavailable, and personal loans become a pipe dream.

Anyone who once worked in manufacturing and has been fired has already discovered to their bitter surprise that they are not qualified to apply for those few jobs in the third millennium that are still performed by human beings and not by machines, and young people in search of their first jobs realize that their universities have done nothing to prepare them to enter this very new environment. Thus, the two ages, young and old, merge in an army of malcontents, a single indistinct mass, bewildered and angry, left snarling out their rage at the keyboard of a computer, incapable of finding a job that isn't part time, temporary, poorly paid, and humiliating.

Everything that once sustained these millions of women and men and kept them inside a society so that they could become its driving force—a job, the ambition to succeed, a better future than the present glittering before their eyes—now no longer exists. By now there are almost five million people, in Italy alone, living in conditions of absolute poverty, lost in a harsh present where the only position available for them is as losers.

So why should this populace of disappointed, betrayed, and impoverished Western voters continue to vote for the representatives of a political approach that is serious-minded, old-fashioned, reasonable, and unfortunately a complete failure? What do they have to lose by choosing to wax enthusiastic over the unreasonable promises of those who tell them that all that needs to be done is to raze to the ground everything that has been built in the past but hasn't worked, so that they can go back to living in the best of all possible worlds?

In Fitzgerald's masterpiece, Gatsby, thrilled and excited at having seen at long last his beloved Daisy again, tells his friend Nick: "Can't repeat the past? Why of course you can! I'm going to fix everything just the way it was before. She'll see."

Ah, it's impossible for me not to side always and inevitably with Jimmy Gatz, the kid from Minnesota who wants to get ahead in life and refuses to accept limitations and will stop at nothing to achieve success: even change his name to Jay Gatsby and fabricate a past of studying at Oxford as long as that will help him to win back the girl he lost; even spend fortunes on spectacular parties just to catch her attention; and even devote all his energy to the impossible task of turning back the hands of time.

I must have read that book a hundred times, and I'll read it again a hundred more, but *The Great Gatsby* is a literary masterpiece, not a political manifesto for 2017.

Do we really want to break everything and see what happens next? Haven't we already had our fill of creative destruction? And what if we realized, after the collapse of Europe and the euro—all it would take is for Italy to leave the Union—that we'd fucked up yet again, and big time?

In God's name, what has become of us Westerners?

When, exactly, did we abandon the idea of being able to face the future as a community? When did we decide to give up our values?

Where is James Truslow Adams's American dream, *that dream of a land in which life should be better and richer and fuller for everyone, with opportunity for each according to ability or achievement*?

What ever became of *the guiding principle of finance* that you were talking about earlier, Guido, *the profound and inalienable reason it was created centuries and centuries ago, which is to procure money for those who wish to invest in the real economy*?

Who has seen Bill Clinton's utopia come to fruition: *the economic benefits of globalization, the political benefits of democracy and human rights, the educational and health benefits of all things modern, from the Internet to the genetic encyclopedia to the mysteries beyond our solar system*?

And what about that *Italy that is more just, more generous to those who are in need, more prosperous and peaceful, more modern and better run, an Italy that plays an active role in Europe and the world* which Silvio Berlusconi foretold from his desk?

How will we ever manage to get that social elevator working again, now that it is stalled on the ground floor of history, completely disassembled? Where has prosperity gone? Where has the sunny future gone? Where has Bono Vox's one world gone? Where has the United States of Europe gone? And where are our betters hiding now, all those eager supporters of globalization who once pontif-icated in the pages of our newspapers? What do they have to say for themselves now?

That last question is one I know how to answer—unfortunately, the only one in the list. The few of them who are still being interviewed today express their con-trition: they now admit that in the past they *may* have advocated the fairy tale of globalization too uncritically, too vociferously. That they were blinded by the enthusi-asm and the promises, because actually, if you look closely, globalization has ultimately created millions of jobless across Europe, along with deflation, and a skyrocketing plague of inequality.

They've finally realized that in our country it's brought poverty, not prosperity, that it's taken away our work and our future and in exchange it has given us poorly sewn rags and days to spend freely chatting in the void of the social networks, and now they struggle frantically to explain that it must be changed, rebalanced, remodulated—they com-pete to find the right verb—because *the middle class has lost confidence and is impoverished and no longer believes in the overall ambition of the West, in the message of freedom and free markets and openness to the world as synonymous with progress.*

And then, they whisper, clearly embarrassed, their last possible argument: the one that claims that globalization rescued a billion people from poverty.

And it's true. This time, it's true. They're right. Whether it's actually a billion is open to discussion, because the number is certainly lower than that, but basically, it's true.

Now, however, they just need to explain that they were kidding earlier, and that the real reason that globalization was imposed on the world was this: to help those billion people.

All we need now is for them to explain, kindly and charitably, that right from the outset the multinationals that were paying them to spread those optimistic fairy tales of theirs throughout the Western world had actually decided to trigger the bloodbath of small businesses and their millions of employees for this one objective, and for that objective alone: to raise one billion Chinese out of poverty.

What dickheads.

Guido

IT WAS MY EXTREME GOOD FORTUNE to be able to get an education at La Sapienza University, Edoardo, studying in the heterodox and nonconformist intellectual workshop that thrived in the 1950s around the teachings of Federico Caffè, and it was from and through those lessons that I learned about and grew up breathing the concept of "political exchange": and that is, the pact, the social contract that exists—and must exist—between the weaker classes, the ones most vulnerable in economic and social terms, and the dominant classes.

It must be a progressive pact, and it must therefore ensure to each of the signatories of that social contract a better future or, in the worst case, at least a steady maintenance of the current conditions, and never a *masochistic exchange*—that's what it was called—which harms the weaker social entities, otherwise, over the long run, the overall stability of the system would be compromised, triggering a massive cascade of costs down the social pyramid.

There is a deep-seated link between an item of clothing sold by one of the fast fashion labels and a smartphone or a personal computer: these are the most glittering gifts that globalization has given to our society, and in the West there are very few people, even in the most disadvantaged social classes, who lack access to them.

These items occupy one of the pans of the theoretical scale that measures the equilibrium of the political exchange described by Caffè, while in the other pan we should put the rights conquered over the course of the twentieth century by those same social classes: a high-quality education available to one and all, universal health care, the right to a job and a home.

Nowadays this equilibrium is seriously compromised: the political exchange has become masochistic. Access to those hard-won rights has been greatly reduced, and in exchange the weaker classes have gained the treacherous and only apparently painless imposition of the horrible barter that replaced the dignity of certain societal conquests with the consolation of being able to buy consumer goods at low cost. Rights in exchange for merchandise. Social safety nets bartered for an illusion of prosperity.

And so it was that the social elevator was smashed.

The walls of the social pyramid have become smooth, and the millions who once made up the working class and the middle class have slid down them in an unstoppable free fall. And even as they were losing their jobs in the manufacturing sector, they were being hypnotized by the mirage of easy access to consumer goods and encouraged to indulge in the great bounty of merchandise, nearly all of it worthless or little more, all of it produced in other countries and available on easy terms of credit.

The architrave of this new order hopes to transform us all into self-entrepreneurs in the sharing economy, all-out consumers, constitutionally indebted, happy children, contented with this masochistic political exchange which we see busily working away every morning, when we put on our clothes or turn on some device to connect to the Web and we're immediately inundated with offers of bric-a-brac and cheap trinkets.

It wasn't supposed to be like this.

The *telematic network*, as we called it in Italy in the 1990s, sprang from a rigorous tradition of anarchy and the genius of a select few, who insisted that it had to be and remain totally free and exempt from all forms of censorship, because its ultimate goal was to free minds and assist in the diffusion and sharing of information and knowledge that had for too long remained hidden, secret, available to only a select few, and only upon payment.

Today, in contrast, it threatens to become the battlefield of huge tech corporations: an immense emporium where you can find everything, but nothing is free; a sort of war zone garrisoned and hypercontrolled at every level, from the most rudimentary Trojan horses to the deadly devices of cybersecurity and mass surveillance denounced by the former CIA and NSA analyst Edward Snowden.

We're light-years away from the concept of the Internet as a brilliant experiment in social cooperation, a concept that pours crystalline from the writings of Aaron Swartz, the revolutionary boy genius who even in middle school had already come up with new tools for online publishing and had courageously dedicated himself to the attempt to advance the debate on how the Internet should treat the problem of copyright, putting forth opinions that were taboo-shattering and controversial, such as, for instance, in 2004 when, at the age of seventeen, inconsolably orphaned of Napster, he claimed that to download a song wasn't the same thing as stealing one because "if I shoplift an album from my local record store, no one else can buy it. But when I download a song, no one loses it and another person gets it. There's no ethical problem."

Swartz believed that intellectual products—especially those available in digital form—should be treated and considered differently from physical objects, and that defending copyright at all costs could become a dangerous thing, because eventually we'll clash with the free spread of knowledge, the very reason the Internet was first devised.

Even if downloading songs over the Internet harmed the sales of record companies, he explained recklessly, it certainly didn't mean it was unethical, because after all "libraries, video rental places, and used book stores (none of which pay the artist) hurt sales too. Is it unethical to use them?"

He said that it was wrong to punish people for undermining "potential sales" with their downloads, since "earthquakes take away potential sales, as do libraries and rental stores and negative reviews. Competitors also take away potential sales. So can talking to your girlfriend."

Aaron Swartz was a Wikipedia enthusiast, and he explained that "Wikipedia's openness isn't a mistake; it's the source of its success." That the volunteers who helped to compile it, proud of belonging to a community, protected it much better than if they'd been paid to do it. That its secret was the work of a community, of "a group of people that took the project as their own and threw themselves into making it succeed," governed by a single watchword: "Ignore all rules."

He said that "Wikipedia's real innovation was the idea of radical collaboration. Instead of having a small group of people work together, it invited the entire world to take part. Instead of assigning tasks, it let anyone work on whatever they wanted, whenever they felt like it. Instead of having someone be in charge, it let people sort things out for themselves."

In July 2008, at the age of twenty-one, Aaron Swartz came to Italy to address a world librarians' conference at the Eremo dei Frati Bianchi (Hermitage of the White Friars or St. Joseph of the Caves) in Cupramontana, near Ancona, and it was from there that he put forth the

Guerilla Open Access Manifesto, where you can read the following: "Information is power. But like all power, there are those who want to keep it for themselves. The world's entire scientific and cultural heritage, published over centuries in books and journals, is increasingly being digitized and locked up by a handful of private corporations."

And he also wrote: "Forcing academics to pay money to read the work of their colleagues? Scanning entire libraries but only allowing the folks at Google to read them? Providing scientific articles to those at elite universities in the First World, but not to children in the Global South? It's outrageous and unacceptable."

And he further wrote: "But sharing [information] isn't immoral—it's a moral imperative. Only those blinded by greed would refuse to let a friend make a copy." And last of all, he states, in the final appeal: "There is no justice in following unjust laws. It's time to come into the light and, in the grand tradition of civil disobedience, declare our opposition to this private theft of public culture. We need to take information, wherever it is stored, make our copies and share them with the world."

He was light-years ahead of the rest of us, Aaron Swartz. Perhaps too far ahead of us. And he came to a sad, very sad end.

His life began to get complicated when one of his laptops was found in a broom closet at MIT in Cambridge, Massachusetts: the computer was downloading files from an archive of academic articles which could be consulted free of charge from MIT's network, but were behind a paywall for everybody else.

He was arrested on the night of January 6, 2011, not far from Harvard's campus, and charged with thirteen federal crimes, carrying a maximum penalty of fifty years in prison and a million-dollar fine.

Even though Swartz never uploaded any of the files to the Internet, the prosecutor decided to throw the book at him and make him the scapegoat, the one who pays for everyone else's sins. He was charged with excessive downloads from a free site, that is, the equivalent of the crime of borrowing too many books from a public library.

Negotiations between his lawyers and Carmen Ortiz, United States attorney for the district of Massachusetts, failed—for that matter, the U.S. attorney had a very different opinion from our main character: "Stealing is stealing whether you use a computer command or a crowbar, and whether you take documents, data or dollars"—and when Aaron Swartz learned that he would be facing trial and that he ran the concrete risk of being sentenced to thirty years in prison, he had a mental breakdown and committed suicide, hanging himself in his Brooklyn apartment.

It was January 11, 2013.

He was twenty-six years old.

Edoardo

AARON SWARTZ WAS ALSO THE ONLY PERSON capable of figuring out the infinitely concealed plot of David Foster Wallace's *Infinite Jest* and explaining it on his blog so that it could be understood by all those who had read the book but hadn't understood it, like me.

Guido

RADICAL COLLABORATION! Who can even remember that idea anymore, now that the Web has been transformed from an instrument of liberation into a means of Orwellian control, which violates all boundaries and eliminates even the concept of privacy?

Plunged into a dystopia, we find ourselves under the unblinking eye of a new surveillance capitalism that battens off the continuous monitoring of digital identities and the accumulation and aggregation of the information spun off by our online behaviors, purchases, and even routes of Internet navigation.

This is big data, the load-bearing beams of an extractive paradigm capable of mining value from every aspect of human life, from knowledge to relationships, language skills to basic needs, in an indefinitely extendable productive cycle that can even transform social networks into a resource. While we think we're chatting freely, our information, preferences, and opinions are archived and made available to—for the advantage of—immense corporations.

Even the mechanisms of sharing have become an opportunity for profit: the sharing economy consists of the common use of a good or the enjoyment of a service, but no matter how sociable and friendly and useful and convenient it may seem, the app that manages the sharing remains private and proprietary, and a substantial chunk of the profit from every sharing transaction is kept by the owner.

The provider of infrastructure or labor—that is, the person who makes available his car or his time or his ability to offer a service—is pleased and proud to feel that he is a free-market entrepreneur of himself and to be able to make money by renting for a short time something that at the end of the service becomes his again, and only rarely does he realize that he has in fact accepted a very grueling form of work upon command that not only occupies all his time and keeps him from performing other work, but also brings him little more than chump change and provides him with absolutely no rights or guarantees.

It's a form of self-exploitation disguised by the deceptive mantra that preaches the transformation of every individual into a company, and creates a labor force that's amateurish and therefore easily extorted, uprooted, and subject to total mobility, which instead of generating new employment opportunities tends to offer low-cost versions of professionals and structures that already exist, ultimately eliminating reliable, long-term jobs, thereby impoverishing society and helping to steer it toward deflation.

In economics textbooks, we read that deflation is the general decline of prices, and therefore the diametrical opposite of inflation and—at first glance—a good and just thing.

Actually, though, deflation is a bad thing, and it's produced by a bad situation, that is, the decline in demand for goods and services and the resulting drop in the prices that companies set in order to lure in the increasingly rare buyers—something that fails to work as often as not, but which certainly has repercussions on a company's balance sheet, with a reduction or complete elimination of profits, whereupon it becomes necessary to cut costs and reduce the labor force. Those workers who are let go return home and stop buying, and the economy goes into a tailspin, diving into recession and remaining there.

Today it is not only the pressure of a nearly decade-long downturn that is crushing down the prices of products and services, but also the convergence of a diverse number of factors. The austerity imposed along with QE, globalization, technological advances, the offshoring of production to countries where the cost of labor is lower, the sharing economy, and even immigration are deflationary factors.

Austerity demands a compression of salaries and consumption which undermines the markets in goods and services, ultimately blocking them. Globalization unleashes worldwide competition for each and every market, and the struggle over prices is the fulcrum of that battle. Every day technology offers new methods for doing work without human intervention, thus driving down the costs of products and services while creating a reservoir of the unemployed who are willing—indeed obliged—to accept any and all conditions of employment and levels of payment, as long as they can work and earn.

It seems to me that you've written quite enough about the impact of offshoring on prices, Edoardo, and the sharing economy was discussed just now. Immigration, moreover, which is so often and so intolerably the cause of tragedies here in Italy, only helps to continually fill to overflowing the reservoir of manpower that is already far greater than demand could ever require.

Welcome to the inferno of deflation, which is after all nothing more than the proper *contrappasso*—to cite Dante's theological version of poetic justice in the damnation of souls for specific sins in his *Inferno*—for those who have lived their whole lives in sacred, unreasoning terror of inflation.

While, in strictly theoretical terms, deflation isn't an unalloyed evil for the weaker classes, since lower prices reduce the cost of living and increase purchasing power, albeit in the presence of a salary that remains fixed, that's not how things work in the real world, because in contrast with all the economic theories that we studied at the university, there is now an elephant in the room. New, immense, never seen before. And invisible, because only a few people know about it. This elephant is QE.

Let me tell you another story.

During the Gold Rush, in America, it became clear that in places where a new vein of gold ore had been discovered, there was soon a greater number of thefts, robberies, and social disorders of all kinds. In defiance of all expectations, in the face of new wealth, the community fractured instead of flourishing, and violence broke out continuously, without restraint.

That's right, because the miners who lived around the new mine suddenly discovered that they were rich, and they started buying up all the goods and services that were then considered essential: the biggest houses, the best doctors, the freshest food, the finest whiskey, the prettiest prostitutes.

For the rest of the community, that is to say, all those who were excluded from the new vein of gold, all those goods suddenly became unattainable, and civil disorder, violence, and uprisings ensued.

Today we might say that the gold mines of yesterday are the central banks of today, while the gold ore is now zero-interest bonds. Only a very few have access to zero-interest money—namely, those who have the power, the political swing, or the assets to offer as collateral—and they are the recipients of rivers of cash, free to run up debt without fear and buy whatever they want, perhaps sheltering that money in investments in sectors regulated by state tariffs.

Those who don't have access to zero-interest money—meaning those who lack power or political swing, or assets to offer as collateral—see the prices drop for things they don't need, like the rags of fast fashion, while the prices of things they have no choice about consuming, such as taxes, tariffs, the costs of school and health care, just keep rising.

And so it is that people slip into poverty. When equal opportunities die. When trenches are dug between social classes. When rights are traded for merchandise, and fundamental goods are swapped for discretionary purchases and impulse buys.

And then, to use the words of an old friend of mine, people get angry, and they don't even know who or what they're angry at.

Edoardo

YOU WERE TALKING ABOUT FAST FASHION earlier, Guido.

I know them, the gentlemen of fast fashion. I know them very well. They used to come see us twice a year.

At the beginning of the season, when we'd show our summer collection and they'd order three or four swatches of fabric to get them copied and manufactured cheaply in China.

And at the end of the season, when work was subsiding, and they'd offer to place a major order for one of our finest and most expensive and most demanding products that, evidently, they hadn't been able to get copied in China.

They'd always explain that they didn't want to pay our list price, that indeed they couldn't afford to, and that they weren't interested in getting that exact fabric anyway: they'd happily make do with a cheaper version of it, one that resembled the original as closely as possible. But much cheaper. Usually about 30 percent cheaper.

Each time we'd reply that it was out of the question, but then, each time, we'd find a way to produce the article requested: it was too important to keep the looms working, instead of letting them sit idle and having to send our employees home on half pay.

We'd work with these gentlemen to change the makeup of the fabric, to adjust the weight, we'd look for cheaper raw materials, we'd wheedle discounts out of our suppliers and our finishers, and in the end we'd deliver a fabric that, perhaps, still had some distant resemblance to the original. They were happy and so were we. Stupidly, so were we.

Guido, I feel sure that someday people will look back and laugh at this full-fledged disease of our thought processes that has metastasized into a universal fixation on diving after the lowest price for any product and any service, with no regard for the concept of quality.

I'm sure that someday people will look back and bitterly pity this downward pressure that compresses all desires, ambitions, activities, expertise, and experience, making us forget that every time we choose the cheaper product instead of the more expensive one, we get less, not more, for our money.

And I'm certain that if the film industry survives the obscene stagnation that awaits it, in ten years or so we'll see irresistible comic films about the childish pleasure with which we hurry to purchase so many things we don't need simply because they cost next to nothing, never considering *how often* we buy all those things that cost next to nothing and are basically worthless.

We'll all come off as fools, and our grandchildren will have every right to make fun of us because, while we were busy defending the rights of the Atlantic bluefin tuna and migratory birds, it never occurred to us to ask who the person was in China or Myanmar or Vietnam who sewed the T-shirt that we bought for five euros, much less wonder how much they were paid, and we never realized that this was a colossal and criminal case of exploitation in which we were fully complicit, because without our purchases it never would have taken place.

They'll depict us hunched over our smartphones, busy commenting on the bullshit that total strangers have posted, with little messages crowded with yellow emoji faces, dressed miserably because we're so incapable by now of distinguishing between the beautiful and the unappealing that we've just decided to ignore the difference entirely, and they'll laugh insanely at what happy victims we were of the vacuous enthusiasm that every great new technology unleashes, the unwitting grandchildren of those heads of household in the 1950s who would put on a jacket and tie to watch television in their living rooms.

They'll laugh at us and ridicule us, and we'll deserve it.

Back then, though, at my family's company, Lanificio T.O. Nesi & Figli S.p.A., those large orders came in handy, even if payment came after 120 days and there wasn't a euro's profit to be had out of the deal. We just told ourselves that it helped to chip away at the company's general expenses and kept us in the good graces of big clients who just kept getting bigger and declaring dozens and dozens of millions of euros of profit—not revenue, *profit*—and in the future—we hoped—might even deign to give us orders that were less challenging and more profitable.

Only it never happened.

They just kept coming every year, those gentlemen, and always and only with the usual intention of bastardizing one of our finest fabrics, and we continued to serve them, and never was that verb more appropriate as a descriptor of the behavior of a company that in the golden years would have just told them all to go soak their heads, they and the brilliantined cutthroats they represented.

Today I read with great satisfaction and admiration about the exploits of those intrepid and tireless activists—and they're nearly always women—who all over Europe struggle to explain to the consuming public that fast fashion (appropriately enough, this name is more reminiscent of hamburgers than fashion) necessarily springs from exploitation and battens off exploitation in order to prosper, because it really isn't possible to offer the prices that these people offer without having wrung someone's neck somewhere down the line — or everyone's neck — in the very long manufacturing chain necessary to produce those rags without history or genius, rags that millions across Europe and around the world line up every week to buy, finding them beautiful, finding them new, finding them fashionable.

Let's follow it, this chain. Let's touch each of its links.

We start with the bottomless poverty of Uruguayan sheepherders or cotton farmers in Turkmenistan. Then we sit down alongside the hundreds of thousands of Chinese and Bengali and Laotian and Cambodian women who cut and stitch from dawn to dusk in filthy, poorly lit shacks, often before they've even turned eighteen. Then let's board the immense cargo ships subject to no nation's laws that ply the oceans of the world, and let's stand guard over the shipping containers packed full of rags. Now we dock in the icy ports of Northern Europe and we stand by watching, unastonished at the total lack of monitoring or inspection as the merchandise clears customs. We offload the containers and we load their contents into vans and we race down highways late at night in order to get those damned rags without history or genius to the stores in time, and then we greet the dawn in the company of the window dressers, who work quickly to dress mannequins with the newly arrived rags, and we throw open the shop doors to the salesclerks, male and female, who are going to sing their praises to the customers. We stand by, awestruck, as the various special sales are announced, with prices cut so low that they skirt the realm of the metaphysical, and we wait with interest to see whether salesclerks are simply posted at the shop's front door to hand out free T-shirts and skirts to passing pedestrians.

And now let's look at ourselves in the mirror when we put one on—one of these damned rags—and let's ask ourselves whether the fact that we're wearing these tremendously undistinguished *schmattes* isn't the most glaring benchmark of the general decline in which we've forced ourselves to live.

It really does strike me as increasingly necessary to give all possible support and encouragement to the conscientious, courteous, and trenchant efforts of these women, intrepid activists all, who tirelessly explain to other young women and young men and girls and boys that buying an article of clothing every week just because it looks new and costs next to nothing only to toss it in the trash after twenty days—that is the European average—is nothing short of a compulsive action, emblematic of a disease of the soul.

Support them, then, in word and deed, as they reveal what's there before our eyes and yet still invisible to us, which is to say, the brilliantly manipulative technique whereby the shopper's attention is focused on the low price paid, while immediately rinsing from their memories any recollection of all the other useless purchases, mostly already discarded, thereby preventing said shopper from ever coming to a final summation of all these purchases; otherwise people would realize that they've already spent a really substantial sum on all the disposable rags they've bought.

Unlike me, they're capable of telling this whole story without once losing their tempers, calmly, with the proper dose of indignation, providing a continual stream of accounts of just what happens in the factories that produce the things we buy, without once venturing into the larger and indeed immense question of ugly products that are palmed off as beautiful, low quality sold as good, the fragile that's proudly declared to be robust, the old counterfeited as new. Or the fundamental lie that sits at the center of this rotten mechanism, and that is, the idea that in those shops it's possible to buy luxury and quality and elegance, and spend just a few euros.

They even manage to hold their tongues when necessary, and if someone tells them even now that they're simply grateful for the chance to dress fashionably while saving lots of money, they refrain from telling them that however it is they're dressed, fashionable it's certainly not.

Because fashion, by God, was something entirely different once.

III. 2016

Guido

AT THE BEGINNING of the scorching summer of 2016, with the Brexit referendum and the American presidential election in November looming imminent, nothing seems capable of unsettling the status quo against which this book has issued its extended and heartfelt jeremiad.

For that matter, if we leave out the abrogation of the Glass-Steagall Act by Bill Clinton in the long-ago year of 1999, none of the many and still very grave political events of the past twenty years have ever had a major and lasting impact on finance and the economy.

In the system that we've been given, the ability of the actions of a single prime minister or a single nation or even a coalition of nations to influence the way markets move now appears reduced to the lowest possible terms. What guides with a firm hand the stock markets and trade of the world is the slow forward progress of immense forces unleashed sixteen years earlier by political and cultural decisions made in the middle of the 1980s by politicians who grew up during the Second World War: those decisions carve out the nature of this world, certainly not the decisions made by the governments currently in power which, at least in the West, struggle mightily to administer the status quo and no longer even dream of changing it.

Even though the polls on Brexit call for an uncertain result, it's hard to imagine the United Kingdom leaving the European Union, and the debate between Leave and Remain seems to unfold without kindling great passions, English style, a reflection of the calm and good humor that, thank God, continue to permeate all things Britannic and seem to militate against sharp deviations from the paths of tradition.

It is only in the last few days of the run-up to the referendum, at least in Italy, that we begin to read in the papers and see on TV accounts that veer away from the usual chorus of praise for the British economy, invariably presented by the correspondents as extremely vital and dynamic, extremely modern and multicultural—probably a reference to the economy of magnificent London, where all the correspondents live.

The stories that start to filter through, instead, tell of a different reality in the British provinces, where outsourcing and offshoring has hit hard, and hundreds of thousands of jobs have fled, and a strong sentiment of malaise has spread, indeed a creeping wave of anger toward everything that represents the United Kingdom's age-old tradition of open doors to the world, immigration included. It would seem that, just as London is busy declaring its enthusiasm about remaining a part of Europe, the rest of England is determined to get out, whatever the cost.

Then, a week before the referendum, a young Labour Party MP campaigning for Remain, Jo Cox, is murdered, stabbed and shot to death by a crazed Nazi who attacks her, shouting *Britain first!* and the world finally turns its worried attention to the United Kingdom, where the latest polls, certainly influenced by the tragedy, give Remain the lead.

The narrow victory of Leave over Remain hits Europe and the markets like a sledgehammer blow, and immediately points to the immense challenge, in both practical and psychological terms, of how to break the United Kingdom away from Europe, politically and economically and financially, because this time there is an established exit procedure—invoking Article 50 of the Treaty on European Union—but it's never been activated before in this way: until now. In fact, nations have always asked to enter the European Union, never to exit it.

A few months later comes Donald Trump's incredible, unthinkable victory in the American elections—polling had predicted that he too was sure to lose, and he too rose to triumph on the vote of the manufacturing states that had most critically hemorrhaged jobs in the post-globalization labor market—to reveal to us the face of an America we didn't know: a country profoundly lacerated and brutally awash in discontent, entirely different from the exultant, future-facing land that we've been spoon-fed by the televisions and newspapers and even by macro-economic data.

We must recognize that not even strong growth (at least by the standards we've become accustomed to in Europe) and declining unemployment are enough to give a picture of the real economic and financial situation of the United States: the fate of its citizens varies too widely, the difference between their visions of the present is too radically different, too unequally distributed the prosperity that the economy still continues to pump out.

The America that we see now is European—far too European—populated not only by those who have managed to understand and interpret the rules of the new globalized world and turn those rules to their own bene-fit, but also inhabited by tens of millions of the defeated, furious victims, whose stories seem to come straight out of a book by Steinbeck, and whom pollsters, evidently, are unable to reach or to measure.

This is a populace whose voice we've never had a chance to hear before, people who live outside the big cities, or who have been expelled from them. These are people who've lost their jobs due to the advent of global-ization and are unable to find new ones, winding up in the grim limbo of those disheartening, extremely unreliable, underpaid jobs that Douglas Coupland in his book *Generation X* called McJobs. These are people who feel disenfranchised of their futures, who can't stand living the lives they lead, and who have apparently decided that Hillary Clinton represents the symbol and the root cause of everything that's wrong with America and their lives.

And so it is Donald Trump—the most unlikely leader of the millions of the disinherited that you could possibly imagine—who takes the oath on January 20, 2017, before the U.S. Capitol, to preserve, protect, and defend the Constitution of the United States, so help him God, and he begins to deliver his inaugural address just as it starts to rain over Washington, and he says:

> For many decades, we've enriched foreign industry at the expense of American industry; subsidized the armies of other countries while allowing for the very sad depletion of our military. We've defended other nations' borders while refusing to defend our own; and spent trillions and trillions of dollars overseas while America's infrastructure has fallen into disrepair and decay.

And then he says:

> We've made other countries rich, while the wealth, strength and confidence of our country has dissipated over the horizon. One by one, the factories shuttered and left our shores, with not even a thought about the millions and millions of American workers that were left behind. The wealth of our middle class has been ripped

from their homes and then redistributed all across the world.

And he goes on to say:

But that is the past. And now, we are looking only to the future. We assembled here today are issuing a new decree to be heard in every city, in every foreign capital, and in every hall of power. From this day forward, a new vision will govern our land. From this day forward, it's going to be only *America first! America first!*

And he continues:

Every decision on trade, on taxes, on immigration, on foreign affairs will be made to benefit American workers and American families. We must protect our borders from the ravages of other countries making our products, stealing our companies and destroying our jobs. Protection will lead to great prosperity and strength. I will fight for you with every breath in my body and I will never ever let you down!

And he says:

America will start winning again, winning like never before. We will bring back our jobs. We will bring back our borders. We will bring back our wealth. And we will bring back our dreams. We will build new roads and highways and bridges and airports and tunnels and railways all across our wonderful nation. We will get our people off of welfare and back to work, rebuilding our country with American hands and American labor.

We will follow two simple rules: *Buy American* and *Hire American*.

And he adds:

We will not fail. Our country will thrive and prosper again. We stand at the birth of a new millennium, ready to unlock the mysteries of space, to free the earth from the miseries of disease, and to harness the energies, industries and technologies of tomorrow.

And this is how he ends his speech, the forty-fifth president of the United States of America:

You will never be ignored again. Your voice, your hopes, and your dreams will define our American destiny. And your courage and goodness and love will forever guide us along the way. Together, we will make America strong again. We will make America wealthy again. We will make America proud again. We will make America safe again. And yes, together we will make America great again. Thank you. God bless you. And God bless America.

PEACEABLE ANIMALS

"CIAO GUIDO, sorry I'm calling so late, but it's important."

"Oh, ciao Edo. No problem. What's up?"

"What's up is that you have to call Elisabetta immediately. I mean right now, this second, it doesn't matter how late it is, and tell her that we're canceling the book contract."

"What? Why?"

"We need to return the advance…Which believe me I'm not happy about, because I've already spent that money, but there's nothing else we can do…"

"Hold on just a minute."

"No, Guido, we can't wait. At the very most, we can take until tomorrow morning. There's no time to lose. Sure, she'll get mad at first, but in the end she'll understand. She always understands everything."

"What is there to understand, though?"

"That we can't turn the book in now."

"But wait, Edo—we've finished it!"

"No, no—"

"But why?"

"What do you mean, why?"

"Are you talking about Trump's speech?"

"Of course! And what, if not that? I watched the whole thing, from when he left the White House with Obama until he flew away in the presidential helicopter...He said things that are exactly the same as the things that we wrote, Guido. But I mean exactly identical. He said that the wealth of our middle class was stolen from our homes and redistributed around the world. He said that it's time to put an end to shuttering factories, only to reopen them in China, time to stop laying off factory workers...He said the same things that we wrote in the book, Guido."

"But he's always said those things."

"Now, what do you think someone like Trump knows about factories and manufacturing and hard work and factory workers? He's never set foot in a factory, he's never seen one, not even from a distance!"

"I know that."

"It's just unbelievable. He's spent his whole life throwing up apartment buildings and he's made his billions and now he claims to be the paladin of small business and blue-collar workers, and he gets elected president—"

"But what does the book have to do with it?"

"It has everything to do with it, because the last thing I want is for anyone to think that he and I—that he and the two of us, you and me—agree on *anything*, because we fucking don't!"

"Of course we don't."

"Because we don't believe that it's a good idea to go back to autarky, seal off our borders. All we want is a fair deal, a level playing field, and that some rules be introduced to regulate this fictional free market, right?"

"Of course."

"I say it as an old free-market liberal. The market has to be regulated. Regulated properly, and regulated as little as possible, of course. But, still, regulated."

"We aren't made for liberty. Even Dostoyevsky said so."

"Listen to the books this money manager has read."

"You're not the only one who's read books, you know..."

"And then there's all those horrible things he says about immigrants, which I find disgusting, and have nothing to do with the decline of the economy. That's something only racists believe, that old chestnut about how immigrants steal jobs, those bastards who hate foreigners and are always looking for excuses to pile on, all the while spouting protestations that they aren't racists.

Because if the economy's growing, then the economic system absorbs immigration easily, if anything immigration reinforces the economy. Like in Prato in the 1970s. I know, because I watched it happen…"

"The same as everywhere else, Edoardo, not just in Prato. Always. The central problem is always the same: growth. A society, a nation, a civilization is healthy as long as it offers its people an opportunity for growth. When that opportunity vanishes, the society falls ill. In the end, it's all right there."

"…"

"…"

"Yes. In the end, it's all right there."

"Edo, listen to me. Trump realized that globalization hasn't worked for the vast majority of people living in the West, and he started saying so with the biggest megaphone in the world. He didn't come up with it and we didn't come up with it. He didn't invent this thing, and it's not even a right-wing idea. It's simple reality, and it's there for anyone to see, in Italy and in Europe and in America. We both just wrote a book about this thing. Right?"

"Right."

"So that's it, that's the only reason Trump won. Because he hit the bull's-eye, he identified the problem."

"He saw the immense problem."

"Exactly, he saw the immense problem, as you put it. And it doesn't matter that he got everything wrong during his campaign, and for that matter it doesn't matter that he has no idea how to solve this immense problem, aside from all the idiotic claptrap he spouts about the old protectionist rhetoric, America First. He pointed out the economic failure of the West, he threw in all the bullshit about immigration, and he found the perfect electoral platform for the times we live in. Then he also had the unbelievable good luck to find himself face-to-face with a weak candidate, an extremely weak candidate, and he beat her. That's how it went."

"Okay, but now what? What happens now?"

"What happens now is that thanks to him and the example he's set, so to speak, there's a good chance that his little friends all over Europe will go on to win elections. I feel as if I've fallen into that poem by Yeats..."

"What was that wonderful line about the falcon?"

"*Turning and turning in the widening gyre, the falcon cannot hear the falconer; things fall apart; the center cannot hold.* But what are you doing still up at this hour of the night? I'm the one who never sleeps..."

"I just can't seem to sleep, Guido. I keep seeing Trump saying the same things that we're saying and I feel like smashing my head against the wall...Luckily now I've found a documentary about narwhals. They're wonderful creatures, practically speaking small horned whales, sea unicorns...It tells the story of this pod of narwhals that's ventured too far north and is trapped among the shifting ice of the North Pole, in a sort of tiny pond...Because they're cetaceans and they need oxygen, just like we do, so they have to take turns surfacing to breathe, and you see all these sharp horns poking up through the ice..."

"I've always wondered what they're for, those horns…"

"No one seems to know. Certainly not to fight, because narwhals are peaceful creatures, and not to kill their prey either…By the way, they have excellent diets, we should follow their example: all they eat is sole, turbot, and Arctic cod…They chase these fish under the ice for miles, but then if they can't find an airhole, they run out of oxygen and drown…And anyway, they aren't horns, they're tusks. A single really long canine tooth, more than six feet long in some cases, made of ivory. It's considered a very precious trophy."

"Why, do they hunt them?"

"Only a very few every year, and only the Inuit, on account of their traditions…A few years ago, an Inuit sent me an email offering me an eight-foot-long narwhal tusk…The price was very high, something like four thousand Canadian dollars, if I remember rightly…It was beautiful. They aren't smooth, you know, they grow in a spiral…"

"And did you buy it?"

"No, but I thought it was interesting to get email from an Inuit. He lived in Nanaimo, in British Columbia, on Vancouver Island, which is right across from the city of Vancouver, where Malcolm Lowry wound up going to live, and where he wrote 'Ghostkeeper,' the short story where we found this thing of ours about the celestial machinery."

"Seriously?"

"Yes. It was Sandro Veronesi who asked me to translate that story, years and years ago, when we were still young…One time we went, he and I, to Vancouver, to find the place where Lowry's cabin was…In Dollarton, just outside of Vancouver, in a stand of century-old fir trees…In the end, we looked and looked until we found the exact spot…It was in a sort of inlet, almost like a fjord, and in the distance you could see the refinery that sent up those infernal flames that so terrified Lowry when he was filthy drunk, which is to say, always…"

"Did you go into the cabin?"

"No, the cabin isn't there anymore. The place burned down on him, poor guy, and he not only lost the cabin, he also lost the manuscript of *In Ballast to the White Sea*, the enormous novel he was writing that was supposed to be the *Paradiso* of a trilogy, with *Under the Volcano* as the *Inferno* and *Lunar Caustic* the *Purgatorio*…"

"And he didn't have a copy?"

"No."

"But didn't he try to rewrite it?"

"He tried, but he couldn't do it. So it's utterly lost."

"Ah, hold on, now I've found the channel, here it is, the documentary about narwhals…And there they are…There's so many of them, and they have to take turns poking up into that tiny hole…There are too many of them, they'll never make it…"

"Yeah, right, there must be a dozen of them, at least…"

"They're prisoners there, how long can they hold out?"

"I don't know, Guido."

"Then why won't anyone help them?"

"What do you mean?"

"Yeah, why don't the documentary crew do anything to help them? The film crew, the producer, I mean everyone's standing around filming while they're in danger of dying and they don't do anything to save them...Why don't they do something? Why don't they break the ice to free them? After all, they got to the Pole in an icebreaker, didn't they?"

"I think so..."

"This isn't one of those tearjerker documentaries that make you fall in love with the animals and then lets them die, is it? Because if it is I really don't want to watch it. I've had a tough day myself, on account of that speech by Trump..."

"Hold on, let's just see what happens..."

"The way they take turns surfacing to breathe is really unbelievable...It's like they're dancing, isn't it?"

"Yes, and then there's all this flashing of horns that aren't horns, weapons that aren't weapons and serve no purpose..."

"Edo, those narwhals are like us. They're prisoners of the ice, just like us. And like us, they're surrounded by an infinite, wonderful ocean, but they can't swim out into it because they've swum into a trap all by themselves..."

"Wait, hold on..."

"You see..."

"They got free!"

"Right."

"They got free. They're not dying after all."

"They're saved."

"Yes. They're saved."

Acknowledgments

WE BOTH OWE OUR THANKS to Elisabetta Sgarbi, as always and for a thousand things, starting with the great adventure of the Nave di Teseo, in which she let us serve as crew, until we came to this book, which grew out of a sort of theatrical production she had us do at the Milanesiana festival.

Guido also wishes to thank the collective idiavoli.com, while I owe my thanks to Carlotta, she too as always, and for a thousand different things.